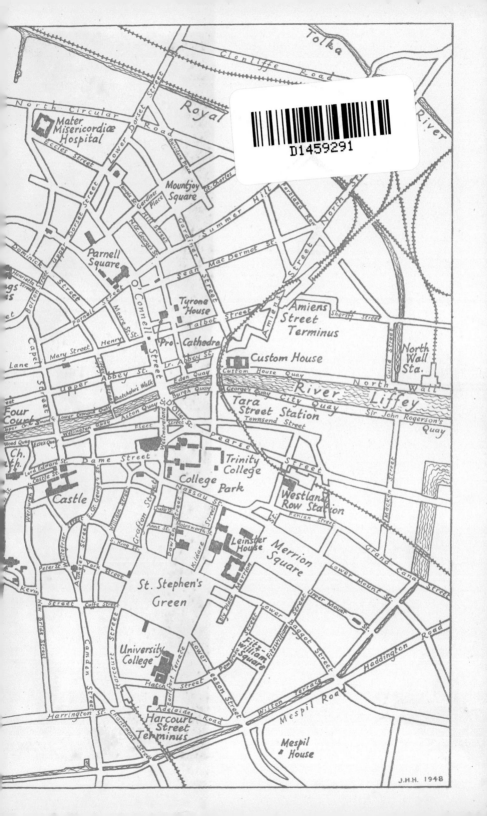

J.H.H. 1948

DUBLIN

1   The Liffey and Four Courts looking towards the sea
From a colour-print by T. S. Roberts, c. 1820

DUBLIN

A Study in Environment

John Harvey

B. T. BATSFORD LTD.

LONDON   NEW YORK

TORONTO

SYDNEY

Other Books by John Harvey

GOTHIC ENGLAND
A Survey of National Culture, 1300–1550

HENRY YEVELE
The Life of an English Architect, *c.* 1320–1400

THE PLANTAGENETS

First published, 1949

2 The Bank of Ireland
From an engraving after G. F. Sargent, c. 1840

MADE AND PRINTED IN GREAT BRITAIN
BY JARROLD AND SONS LTD., NORWICH, FOR THE PUBLISHERS B. T. BATSFORD LTD.,
LONDON : 15 NORTH AUDLEY STREET, W.1 AND MALVERN WELLS, WORCESTERSHIRE
NEW YORK : 122 EAST 55TH STREET   TORONTO : 480–6 UNIVERSITY AVENUE
SYDNEY : 156 CASTLEREAGH STREET

Contents

3 Parliament Square, Trinity College
From an engraving after G. F. Sargent, c. 1840

Acknowledgment

THE author and publishers here express their indebtedness to the following persons and institutions for the illustrations mentioned: Aer Lingus for Fig. 117; the late Anthony Ayscough (by courtesy of Messrs. Heywood Hill) for Figs. 139, 140, 141; Messrs. Black Star Ltd., for Figs. 37, 52, 58, 85, 121; the Syndics of the Cambridge University Press for Fig. 35 (from G. Fletcher: *Leinster East and West*, 1922); Mr. J. Allan Cash, F.R.P.S., for Figs. 36, 37, 49, 52, 54, 55, 58, 79, 83, 85, 86, 121; Mr. Bernard Cox, A.R.I.B.A., for Figs. 41, 43, 99; Mr. R. Deegan, F.R.P.S., Dublin, for Figs. 11, 14, 15, 27, 40, 61, 71, 74, 100, 115, 153, 159, 160; Messrs. Dorien Leigh for Figs. 28, 131; the Lord Herbert for Fig. 135; Irish Press for Fig. 25; the Irish Tourist Association for Figs. 16, 20, 34, 42, 44, 51, 107; Messrs. Judges Ltd., Hastings, for Figs. 50, 60; Mr. T. H. Mason, M.R.I.A., Dublin, for Figs. 13, 24, 33, 48, 66, 68, 69, 77, 78, 84, 96, 97, 102, 103, 104, 112, 119, 120, 122, 127, 128, 146, 147, 149, 150, 151, 152, 154, 155, 156, 161; the Municipal Gallery of Modern Art, Dublin, for Fig. 111; the National Gallery of Ireland for Figs. 1, 4, 19, 108, 109, 110, 129; the National Library of Ireland for Figs. 23, 32, 56, 80, 118, 142, 144, 148, 157 (all from the Lawrence Collection); for Figs. 137, 138 (both from the Murray Collection); for Figs. 53, 158 (both from photostats of drawings in the collection of the Marquess of Headfort); and for Figs. 5, 6, 22, 30, 38, 39, 59, 64, 78, 81, 89, 136; the National Portrait Gallery, London, for Fig. 133; Mr. Anthony Panting for Figs. 7, 18, 29, 57, 65, 67, 93, 94, 95, 101, 105, 106, 114; the late Will F. Taylor for Fig. 143; Miss P. Thompson, A.R.P.S., Dublin, for Figs. 12, 21, 73, 75, 82, 116, 132, 134, 145; Messrs. Valentine & Co. for Fig. 26; and the Victoria & Albert Museum for Figs. 45, 70, 76.

Figs. 46, 47, 87, 88, 92, 98, 123, 124, 125, 126 and the front endpaper are from drawings by the author, based on the Ordnance Survey Maps by permission of Oifig na Suirbhéireachta Ordonáis, Dublin. The back endpaper is from the map by John Rocque, 1756. Figs. 2 and 3 are from Mr. and Mrs. S. C. Hall: *Ireland*, 1841–43; and Figs. 10, 17, 31, 130 are from the publishers' collection.

Preface

DUBLIN is still a city almost unknown to English people, and the loss is ours. Between the mountains and the sea, it is one of the most fortunate of European capitals, and it has the enormous advantage of consisting mainly of buildings produced at the peak of its historic culture. Even English lovers of Georgian architecture, fond of England's rather colourless austerity, are a little frightened of the exuberance of Dublin—the rich and coloured traces of a southern, catholic, baroque past, that England never knew. We English have to go right back to the Middle Ages to find a period when we were fully alive, vitalised with rude health and abounding in a sense of the brilliant poignancy of life. Our eighteenth century consisted too largely of a formal and negative taste, without deep roots, and based on a selfish and cynical philosophy. The culmination of the Renaissance centuries, Georgian England surpassed them in its hollowness.

This is not true of the grand culture of Ireland, nor of Dublin, where life still keeps the full flavour of humanity—a spark which it has never lost. Superficially, much can be explained by differences of race and religion, but there is a great deal more than that in this extraordinary difference between Dublin and, for example, London. Dublin is a phenomenon, and its significance is extraordinary. We may know something of its history, and rather too well the stock phrases of those who have never seen it, and regard Dublin as the chief village of a weird, barbarous, sometimes amusing, but intensely aggravating native tribe. But except for the justifiable panegyrics of the *Official Guide*, we should go a long way before meeting a full realization of just how remarkable Dublin's position is, and how strange.

In the whole of western Europe outside Italy there have, since the fifteenth century, been only three cities with a truly metropolitan stream of culture: Vienna, Paris, London. But Dublin, even if she just misses this rank, comes nearer than any other to it, and has besides the glory of having provided London with a surprisingly large proportion of its cultural equipment. Because of the overwhelming stature of Shakespeare, London's greatest contribution may be said to be the drama, and especially the romantic comedy: Shakespeare's supporting cast, however, would be insignificant if we removed the names of William Congreve, Oliver Goldsmith, Richard Brinsley Sheridan, and George Bernard Shaw, all Dubliners by birth or education. How much English prose literature would be weakened by the loss of Swift, Steele and Burke, and the Irish childhood of Sterne.

In more recent times, Dublin has been the origin or source of inspiration of W. B. Yeats, commonly regarded as the greatest poet of his time; of Oscar Wilde; and of George Moore, the greatest prose writer in English at the turn of the century. The colloquial drama and the descriptive essay received new impetus from the pen of Synge, and George Russell and James Stephens were also bright luminaries of that Irish Literary Revival which has been among the rare symptoms of promise in the twentieth-century world. Among the spiritual progeny of Dublin overseas is Eugene O'Neill. And then there was James Joyce (**108**).

Before passing on to Joyce and the making of books, I will conclude the subject of Dublin's significant standing with a few points from the official guide. Dublin has the oldest maternity hospital, the oldest chamber of commerce, the oldest male voice choral society, and the largest brewery in the world. Its Zoological Garden is the second oldest (two years younger than London) of the modern foundations of its type, though there have been menageries in the world for three thousand years or more. And maybe of greater importance, its Municipal Gallery was the first in the British Isles to be devoted, not to dead and gone, but to modern art.

Modern art, contemporary art, is after all the crux of the problem. In the nature of things no one can be sure which art is going to live on, which will die. But it is relatively easy to pick out a body of work which has the elements of technique and style—and the collection of such bodies of work, that they may receive due study and proper appraisement, is the much needed function of institutions such as galleries of modern art. Dublin led the way, so far as Britain is concerned, and though slowly, the lesson is being learnt. Long ago, Dublin led the way in enthusiastic recognition of Handel's

Messiah, when the composer had been frozen out of England by the patronage cliquery of the time. And the really interesting thing is this, that the Dublin newspaper report of the very first performance alluded to the exquisite delight afforded to the admiring audience, to "the Sublime, the Grand, and the Tender" conspiring to transport and charm the ravished Heart and Ear.

Dublin has had the elasticity to move forward and also backward (she has the only Palestrina Choir outside Rome) in her appreciation of music; England has only added Mendelssohn's *Elijah* to *The Messiah*. Not that I would belittle the enormous strides in English musical appreciation of late years, or the genius of Sir Thomas Beecham, the English dictator. Yet the spontaneous recognition of new works is a faculty which the modern world seems to have lost: it is difficult to recognize in the crawling Edwardianism* of present-day English life the people that called for more Falstaff and applauded the newest symphonies of Haydn.

The fault is not altogether with the public. Ever since the Romantic Movement, ever since the spiritual wrestlings of Shelley and the agonized complaints of Keats, the artist has been putting himself on a pedestal, building himself a house apart. In some cases he has become ashamed of technique, of actual doing; in others he has found it advisable to pretend to a similar foible. W. S. Gilbert thought the term "playwright" a positive insult; he was nothing less than a dramatist. A poet is a maker, a wright whose material is words; nothing more and nothing less, but for the individuality of the spirit which breathes through him. Michelangelo was an universal artist; but he was also a stone-hewer who could be set to cutting cannon-balls. The exquisite paintings of the Middle Ages, the Wilton Diptych and the rest, were produced by men who were admirably trained and equipped house-decorators in their background.

It is quite true, as Dr. Herbert Read has said, that the great painters painted because they "had something serious to say to men and women of refined sensibility and mature intelligence"; but it is a pity to lay too much emphasis on the word "serious" and to exclude other considerations. The artist, like other men, has to live and very often to support a family. It is no good setting up a cry of: I want a patron,

* Edward Elder, Martyr, I, II, III, IV and VIII always excepted.

PREFACE

I cannot demean myself by painting or writing what people will pay for in hard cash. There is in this attitude a peculiarly revolting kind of snobbery and insincerity. Among other objectionable features in it are the assumptions that the public will only pay for tripe, and that the artist is the only man with standards of common honesty. Shakespeare's plays, Mozart's operas, and Dickens' novels are none the worse because their authors were working for their living in writing them. In fact they are better, because they never lose touch with reality.

This is not the same thing as writing down to the masses: Dickens had a nauseating vein of democratic sentimentality, but it is difficult to believe that it was other than a part of his own essential nature. George Moore, who prided himself on refusing to write down to what was supposed to be the popular taste, only discovered his talent for writing English when the Land League agitation had cut off the greater part of his unearned income. Had it not been for the Land League, Moore would probably have wasted himself in the dissipations of Paris. Moore incidentally, in his later days of prosperity, was one of the little group of patrons who sent support to James Joyce, exiled in Switzerland by the war of 1914–18.

Joyce had already shown great literary mastery in his early poems and in *Dubliners*, followed by *A Portrait of the Artist as a Young Man*. There was no question of his potential significance to English literature, but for the remaining twenty-five years of his life he buried himself in the production of the two further, immensely long and increasingly complicated studies of Dublin and Dublin life, *Ulysses* and *Finnegan's Wake*. The final development of Joyce's style, full of admirably bombastic sound-effects, among which the concluding sentences of "Anna Livia Plurabelle" are the best known, removed itself so far from the common man that it ceases to be literature at all; it has sound, sometimes quite magnificent sound, but except by means of prolonged and tedious research and decipherment, sound unlinked to sense.

In the meantime, there stole upon an astonished world an utterly different work, linked to Joyce only by a common origin in Ireland. This book, now famous in its English translation as *Twenty Years A-growing*, was written in Irish for a small circle of Irish speakers on Blasket Island by young Maurice O'Sullivan, one of themselves. Unless the translation has most signally improved upon the original, we may say that a new literature has dawned. Here is the justification of the pathetic attempts of George Moore and his friends to re-awaken the Irish language in Leinster; and more striking, it exactly fulfils Moore's prophetic remark that the Irish language could only be revived by the appearance of a great writer among the peasants of the islands, an Irish Homer. Moore evidently thought this a ridiculous notion, but how its fulfilment would have pleased his sense of the mysteriously appropriate workings of Providence.

Both Moore and O'Sullivan, the one writing in a language he believed to be dying, and the other in one just starting a new lease of life, demonstrate the grand qualities of simplicity and clarity. Moore achieved his end consciously and with a high degree of artifice; but the result contains no obscurities in themselves highbrow or artificial—every sentence can be read by the plain man. Lord Dunsany in one of his autobiographies strings together a series of fine-sounding lines of verse; and then points out that they are not poetry because they convey no connected meaning. This is a very just criticism upon a deal of modern literature and modern art; and it was Moore again who, for all his Parisian background, never ceased to tilt against the paltry preference of so many English writers for French words and phrases.

England can learn a great deal from the historic Irishmen, and from the way in which Irish life is lived. Formality, convention, petty hypocrisy, are all foreign to Dubliners, whose savage repartee springs from a keen delight in verbal wit, and from no spiteful desire to wound. English myself, I say this with affectionate memories of my visits to Dublin, and warmed by lifelong friendship with Dubliners. If dedications were not so frequently false coin, this book would be inscribed to a dear lady of Dublin, friend of my childhood and still my friend, who is known to a wide family "by adoption" as Aunt Evelyn.

I owe a debt of gratitude to my father and mother for taking me to Ireland in early years, and for surrounding me with Irish friends. More immediately, this book has profited from the suggestions and criticism of my wife, whose leavening of Irish blood supplies a deficiency in my own constitution. Thanks are also due to Mr. and Mrs. Harold G. Leask, and to Mr. and Mrs. Thomas H. Mason, for great hospitality and

PREFACE

kindness, as well as for valuable information and advice. For other assistance I am indebted to the Very Rev. E. H. Lewis-Crosby, Dean of Christ Church, Dublin; to Dr. Hayes, Director of the National Library, and to his assistants, especially Mr. P. Henchy; to the Vice-Provost of Trinity College, Dublin, and the Library staff there; to Mr. Conor O'Brien; to Mr. Maurice J. Craig; to Mr. Patrick Meehan, Hon. Secretary of the Old Dublin Society; to Mr. Henry Kennedy, Secretary of the Irish Agricultural Organisation Society Ltd., for permission to visit The Plunkett House; to the Commissioner of An Garda Siochana, for permission to visit the Royal Hospital, Kilmainham, and to his staff and that of the Board of Works, my courteous guides there; and to Mr. Henry A. Vernon, Agent to the Pembroke Estates, and his assistant Mr. F. Biddulph, who kindly showed me their valuable collection of early estate plans. I have also to acknowledge the kindness of Mr. Douglas Goldring in allowing me to quote from his pseudonymously published work *Dublin Explorations and Reflections*.

Finally, I would tender thanks to the many unknown Dubliners who went out of their way to help me; and to my publishers, who made the book possible, and have spared no trouble in its production.

JOHN HARVEY

HALF MOON COTTAGE
BOOKHAM, SURREY
12 *January*, 1949

4 Trinity College Museum
From a print by W. B. Taylor, 1819

5 A Fellow   6 A Fellow-Commoner

DUBLIN ACADEMICAL COSTUME IN 1820
From prints by W. B. Taylor

7　The Goldsmith statue by John Foley in front of Trinity College

I
Towards Dublin

TWO LITTLE WHITE SPOTS SPARKLING IN THE SUN AGAINST blue sea water, resolving before the eyes of a delighted boy into two topsail schooners wafted down St. George's Channel, are the first prelude to Dublin that I remember. My first visit, in infancy and well before the war of 1914–18, I cannot recall. But that second journey in the brilliant summer of 1919, when the war was past and the violence of the troubles was still to come upon Ireland, is still a sharp, clear memory. The great lions of the Menai Bridge, the disappointing darkness of its rumbling interior, the crags of Holy Island, all are ineffaceable preliminaries to the first sea voyage I could understand.

In that voyage I discovered two constants in my own temperament as a traveller: that I am a good sailor in the accepted sense of the phrase, and that I find travel by steamer unutterably boring. Only the revelation of those two little traders with their anachronistic sails made up to me for the grinding monotony of hours at sea, hours which I would so gladly have spent on their decks, or in a train upon a land voyage. But there was a real thrill in the Wicklow Hills rising up from the great curve of the sea, and the more immediate bulk of Howth and the islands of Lambay and Ireland's Eye. Finally the arrival at Kingstown (**20**), with friends on the pier to greet us and take us into Dublin; and for me the alluring discovery of the broad-gauge Irish railways, with their easy smooth-running trains.

The broad-gauge train and the jaunting-car are both symbols of the leisurely and gentlemanly character of Ireland; for if it be true that a gentleman is one who is never in a hurry, there must be more gentlemen left in Ireland than anywhere else in the western world. In the good old days before wars and troubles and customs barriers exhausted the tempers and purses of mankind, you could step ashore at Kingstown off the boat and straight into a through railway carriage for almost any part of Ireland. By the Loop Lines you were connected to the appropriate Mail Train and whisked away without undue haste or any inconvenience at all. And even now in this year of disgrace and degradation 1948, with fuel emergency reducing the Eire time-tables to a page or so, access to Ireland is a great deal more convenient than it is to most places.

If you are not a lover of the petrol engine it is still possible to take a cab, drawn by a horse and driven by a human being, from the end of the pier at Dun Laoghaire or from Westland Row Station in Dublin. For in spite of aeroplanes and automobiles (a car in Ireland means the outside jaunting car, or anything down to a perambulator), this is the last western stronghold of Swift's noble Houyhnhnm, the horse. Fortunately, Ireland is a poor country with limited resources; there are compensations in the fact that she does not possess great oil-gushers and that even the Shannon Scheme cannot wholly electrify the country. So long as Eire continues to resist the blandishments of the moneylenders who would so dearly love to improve her, and sticks to her own way of life, she will continue to be what she always was, a forgotten tower of refuge waiting to save what of Europe is worth saving.

Whatever may be the special virtues of the American Continent (and Latin America may well dominate the next Age), it is too far off to share in the essence of Europe. And there has been something of real value in Europe for about three thousand years—the spark of real humanism. Because of its geographical situation, Ireland has at different periods received the escaping exiles of crushed cultures, and from time to time the world gets back its debt with interest. Ireland is a kind of reservoir performing an essential function in times of danger and destruction. In the present state of human affairs the existence of such a reservoir is of the first importance.

In periods of peace and prosperity great empires should hold sway, reducing frontiers to a minimum. That elder generation which was able to travel throughout western Europe without a passport must naturally regret, as who does not, the passing of an age of comfort and security—an age which in spite of insistence on its own material perfections, was not altogether devoid of a spirit of greatness. But we who have survived a period of cave-shelters and gas-masks, concentration camps and suspension of habeas corpus and secret police, have come to realize that a frontier is not merely an infernal

8   The Blue-Coat School, 1773–83, designed by Thomas Ivory
From the print by James Malton

9   Trinity College with the Provost's Lodge, 1760
From the print by James Malton

10   Trinity College Library, 1712-32
Thomas Burgh, architect

11   Interior of Trinity College Library

nuisance; it can also be a buckler of defence and a restorer of sanity to hurt minds. We think kindly of those who, even in a previous dispensation, chanted the watchword:

> On no condition is extradition
> Allowed in Callao.

The most terrible symptoms of the disease from which mankind now suffers are fear and its companion, suspicion; and we must welcome whatever offers some palliation, even if no cure, for these symptoms. The city of refuge and the right of sanctuary depended in past ages upon a spiritual sanction: even among wicked and abandoned men, a majority feared to violate these safeguards of the criminal, the unfortunate, and the persecuted. Our own period, and this possibly is at the root of its unhealthy state, has lost the fear of God. No restraint is set upon man's fertile invention, even by the fear of material consequences. Only considerations of convenience are likely for the time to avail; and it is fortunate that geographical accident and belligerent convenience should have conspired with pacific determination—to save the neutrality of a few small nations, including Eire.

War is a form, possibly the most dreadful form, of human insanity, and within the walls of the frowning asylum which it builds, no sane thought can live. Even the pacifist and the war-resister, driven into over-emphasis by persecution, do not escape the mental and moral infection altogether. And so it is to the few remaining neutral countries that we have to look for the continuance of undistorted human values. Such values, in the modern world, are largely concentrated in a few great capital cities, more especially in the capitals of the few world languages, of which English is now the chief.

Of all the English-speaking capitals, Dublin alone was not involved in the war of 1939–45. This in itself would give to Dublin, and through it to Eire as a whole, a new and unprecedented importance in the period of post-war reconstruction and development. Of the other neutral capitals of the Second War, Stockholm, Berne, Lisbon, Madrid, only Madrid is also the capital of a great language, and by reason of long civil war only ended in 1939 Madrid was itself in no condition to act as guardian of cultural values. So it is Dublin that at the present moment holds in its hands the future of European thought and the European way of life, just as the Irish airports have become the pivot of international communication. In an earlier Dark Age which began just fifteen hundred years ago, Ireland preserved the dying flame of the classic world, and in cherishing it became herself the first of the modern nations. Now, as the youngest and smallest of them all, she may fulfil this role for a second time.

However much Eire's neutrality owed to accidental factors, it could not in the last resort have been maintained except by a heroic determination grounded in Faith: a heroism and a faith greater, I venture to think, than those animating any of the belligerents. Anyone who wants to sneer at the Irish Premier's maintenance of neutrality should remember that Mr. De Valera has himself been an agitator, a rebel, and a condemned traitor under sentence of death. Unless such a man were morally as well as politically a very great villain, he could not but be animated by some deep and abiding principle. That this is indeed the case is widely admitted by Mr. De Valera's opponents, and the policy of neutrality at least was staunchly supported by all parties.

This is not a book of politics, but they cannot be avoided in Ireland. The policies of the Irish parties are none of my business, but I cannot help knowing something of the deeper questions which have for a century past, and still do agitate the Irish scene. For the reader who may not have followed the Irish problem, and who perhaps regards the Irish as vociferous nuisances rather like the Zionists, I will attempt a very brief sketch of the position. Like the problem of Palestine, that of Ireland is three-cornered: there are two main bodies of internal opinion, and one external, that is, the English. As an Englishman I may be suspected of partisan standing, but I am at least trying to state the case in a fair light and as impartially as may be.

In early ages Ireland was invaded by several different peoples, but over two thousand years ago the country was already organized into sub-kingdoms under a chief king, comparable to the Bretwalda who was paramount over the Saxon Heptarchy in England. There was a remarkably high civilization in early Ireland, and this culture was not interrupted by a Roman Conquest. At the barbarian invasions of Western Europe, Ireland was still a flourishing, independent country: quite suddenly it accepted Christianity, and gave a welcome to the learned and religious refugees from Dark Age collapse.

When the storm was blowing over, the countries of Western Europe, not even excepting Italy, received back the highest elements of their past by means of missionaries and artists from Ireland. Ireland passed through a great creative epoch of art, and all her peoples had adopted one language, whose modern Irish and Scottish forms still survive, in addition to their "colonial" offshoot, Manx.

The Danish and Norse invasions of Europe did not spare Ireland, and permanent Viking towns were set up—at Dublin, Wexford, Waterford, Cork and Limerick, besides smaller places. The Viking King of Dublin, though his own territory did not extend far, became of predominant importance and for a time acquired the prestige that had belonged to the Ard-Rí or paramount King. From the time that Dublin became a permanent trading-post of the "Ostmen" in A.D. 852, it was a centre of Scandinavian exploration, and though there was extensive intermarriage with the Irish, the language remained Scandinavian. Dublin was a foreign settlement at the focal point of Ireland, and this position was maintained for over a thousand years. The invasion by Normans from England substituted Norman-French for Danish, and led to penetration of the country by families of Norman adventurers; later on, as in England, the English language gradually ousted French as the everyday tongue of the invaders, who had in any case been reinforced by English colonists from Bristol. The whole history of Dublin as a capital city for Ireland, and centre of exploitation of Ireland, is bound up with the Danish, Norman, and English settlers from overseas.

The petty wars of the Middle Ages were between neighbouring princes and seldom of a mainly racial or "national" character; but through the fourteenth and fifteenth centuries and even later, the Irish constantly pressed in upon Dublin and kept the "Pale" or area of English settlement tightly penned in. The confused events of the sixteenth and seventeenth centuries materially changed the situation: instead of the Irish pressing in the Pale, the English extended their colonization of the backlands, and "planted" whole counties, to the detriment of the natives. Finally, Oliver Cromwell carried out with bloodthirsty ferocity a plantation of almost the whole of Ireland with English Roundhead soldiery. The Elizabethan and later plantations brought in a new element of contention, for the settlers were Protestants of an extreme

5

type, while the Irish as a whole had retained Roman Catholicism.*

Penal laws allowed only Protestants to hold office and landed estates, and the Irish became a subordinate and impoverished tenantry, though still a vast majority of the population throughout the country except in the extreme north-eastern part of Ulster, which had been solidly settled with Presbyterian Scots a century or so back. Meanwhile, the eighteenth century witnessed the development of a breach between the English government and the Anglo-Norman Protestant "Ascendancy" in Ireland. England, weakened by the War of American Independence, had to grant autonomy to the Irish Parliament in 1783. The seventeen years which followed, until the Union of 1800 abolished the Dublin Parliament altogether, were the high-water of Dublin as a prosperous and cultured capital city. It was a splendid period, but its early collapse was due largely to the fact that it rested on the small Anglican party, repugnant to the Catholic masses, and to the Nonconformist Protestants, from whom sprang Wolfe Tone, the founder of Irish Republicanism.

The Union and the Napoleonic Wars for a time diverted attention from political issues to the problem of religion, and the outcome was the Emancipation of Catholics in 1829, after a prolonged struggle under the leadership of Daniel O'Connell; the whole complexion of Irish affairs was changed, for the Catholic franchise meant that everywhere but in the far North-East the English and Anglo-Norman interest was a small minority. As the nineteenth century went on, three great issues unfolded themselves. First came the campaign of Catholicism to establish itself on terms of full equality in culture and visible show with the entrenched Ascendancy; secondly the agrarian struggle of Irish tenants to free themselves from the control of the great landlords (almost all Protestants); lastly the life or death of the Irish language as a symbol of regenerate nationalism.

At the time, over a period of several generations, the obvious grouping of these issues into two main parties was not clearly seen. Roughly it was true that Catholicism, Irish agrarianism and Home Rule politics, and the Gaelic revival were banded together against the Protestant Ascendancy, the landlords backed by England, and the English language and

* Throughout this book, "Catholic" means Roman Catholic.

12   Charlemont House, 1762-5; now the Municipal
Gallery of Modern Art
Sir William Chambers, architect

13   Aldborough House, 1793-6
Sir William Chambers, architect

14 Statue over East
Portico, 1785

15 Trophy in Foster Place

THE BANK OF IRELAND

16 King's Inns

17 Custom House

THE ROYAL ARMS, DESIGNED BY JAMES GANDON

allegiance, but this division was far from being universal. The founding of the Sinn Féin party early in the twentieth century was in fact the first serious attempt at crystallization along these lines. The constitutional Nationalist Party was at last nearing its goal, and the Home Rule Bill on the point of becoming law when the European war broke out in 1914. Opposition to the measure in the extreme north-east had gone to the lengths of large-scale gun-running with a view to armed insurrection against Irish Rule if the Bill became law and a Dublin Parliament were set up. This led to opposition gun-running on the part of the more extreme Home-Rulers, and to the loss of civilian lives in Dublin when British troops fired upon a party of the nationalist Irish Volunteers in July 1914. The belligerent attitude of the north, and this dreadful incident horrified all but the most bigoted Unionist opinion, and but for the outbreak of war, there would in 1914 have been a settlement at least as satisfactory as that of 1922. And many precious lives would have been saved and lasting bitterness avoided.

The aggrieved minority in 1914 was comparatively small, and apart from English civil servants, few would have left the country. But after the terrible incidents of the 1916 Rebellion and of the two Civil Wars of 1921 and 1922, resulting in appalling losses of civilian life and property, it was inevitable that the new Ireland should have an uphill task. Many non-political Irishmen and women, who were Irish in their broader sympathies though loyal to the British connexion, became exiles. A moderate element between the political extremists, these people could be ill spared, and luckily a considerable number decided to brave the storm. Those who were wise enough to stay, and fortunate enough to survive the troubles, have been loyal to the new dispensation, and have encouraged the liberal and unsectarian policy of the governments of the Free State and of Eire.

In spite of the weakening of the old Protestant Ascendancy, there are still within Eire smouldering embers of the party passions of 1916–22; the northern armed sedition masquerading as loyalism of 1914 and the misery of hope deferred worked like madness in the brains of the fervently sincere young patriots who let loose upon each other and their country, as well as upon their enemies, the miseries of six years of revolution and conflict. Extreme patriotism is not always the refuge of scoundrels; there were probably very few characters, certainly no politicians, as noble and disinterested in their time as were Patrick Pearse and his fellow-martyrs, Roger Casement, Michael Collins (**19**), and Erskine Childers. But they had lost the sense of balance which is so essential for any kind of normal life, and their tragic deaths have invested them with an abnormal and disproportionate prestige.

This cult of the "rebels" will inevitably continue as long as the farcical partition of Ireland continues. I say farcical, not because I think all the right is with the south; any outsider looking at the map or going over the ground can see that there is no conceivable basis for a frontier in the facts of topography, and the area concerned is too small to have significance except as an armed British bridgehead in a potentially hostile country. But the facts of geography demand that the British Isles should be treated as a group of mutually friendly units. What form of association should be adopted is not for me to say, though I think that in the long run a purely personal union under one King with several national Parliaments might prove more acceptable than a federalism which placed the actual seat of government in London.

Even most northerners realize that Dublin is the capital of the whole nation, while Belfast is just a heavily industrialized provincial town with a temporary political importance. What is eventually to be done with the not inconsiderable minority of intransigents whose motto is "No surrender", would puzzle the wisest statesmen. It may be that they will one day find themselves driven into the arms of Dublin by a common detestation of English state socialism; and the liberal policy of the sometime "Free State" in its bitter early years is a good enough guarantee that the fears of the north are largely imaginary. But if Scottish Nationalism receives further impetus from similar causes, and succeeds in regaining some degree of real home rule, Dublin and Edinburgh might find a happier permanent solution by agreeing to exchange the majority populations of Belfast and Glasgow. Religious differences and prejudices remain strong in Ireland, and go deeper than the apparent political contrast between north and south; but to me it seems that these prejudices are weakening as the younger generation grows up, in Ireland as everywhere else. A day will come when all Ireland will be reunited.

But united in the years 1939–45 it was not and could not

8

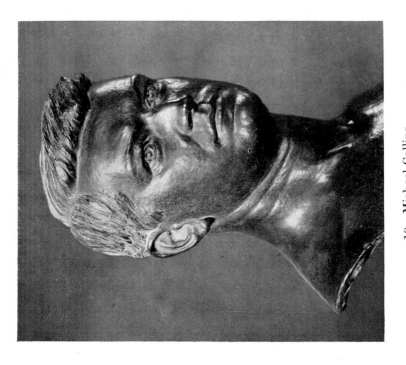

19 Michael Collins
From the bust by F. Doyle Jones

18 James Clarence Mangan
From the bust in St. Stephen's Green

20   Kingstown Station, 1854

21   Broadstone Station, 1850
John Skipton Mulvany, architect

be; apart from the different spectacles through which the two
parties viewed British policy, a move by Eire in either direction spelt disaster. Had Mr. De Valera entered the war as
England's, or even as America's ally, it would have called
forth a new Irish rebellion as surely as Redmond's gesture to
England in 1914 killed the old Nationalist party and opened
the way to Sinn Féin. On the other hand, any attempt to
use the Axis as a lever to end partition would have precipi-
tated a British invasion, the consequent sufferings of an
occupied country at the hands of both sides, and quite
probably the loss of that degree of independence already
attained. When the Axis defeat finally appeared certain, Mr.
De Valera took the very proper line that there was to be no
"jumping on the band wagon".

With the war at its height, there was naturally little English
comprehension of the Eire standpoint. But it was unfortunate that the occasion of final victory should have been made
by Mr. Winston Churchill into an opportunity for a bitter
attack on Eire's neutrality. His broadcast, boasting of the
British Government's wartime "restraint and poise" in not
occupying Southern Ireland was lacking both in sportsman-
ship and sense. The Irish leader's reply, an unexpected
masterpiece of deep but never savage irony, was one of the
outstanding orations of history, and delighted all who were
not completely insulated by party spleen. Reprinted in book-
let form from the "Irish Press" of the 17th May 1945, at the
price of one penny, it continues to be a Dublin best-seller,
with other matter likely to astonish the crowds of English
tourists. After eight years in blinkers, it is startling to see
windows full of the case against English rule, and dozens of
books and pamphlets containing the history and biography
of Ireland's fight for freedom—against England.

There is genuine freedom of the press, for pro-British
sympathy is also expressed, and books and press references
concerning the British Royal Family and their doings are
numerous. Other books of reminiscences, violently anti-
Home-Rule, by former Civil Servants of the old régime are
also well displayed, and are reviewed at length in the Irish
papers. There is no sign in Ireland of that terrible weapon
the conspiracy of silence, used against Aubrey Beardsley fifty
years ago, and more recently, too. Irishmen are too loquacious
and argumentative to be interested in mere suppression of an

opponent. An Irish enemy will gladly proceed from words to wounds and from phrases to fisticuffs, but never deny your existence. This is a part of that spirit, and high spirits, so much more abundant in Ireland than in the rest of the British Isles. Anybody may, and very likely will, come out with an impudence or a repartee too apt and too witty to be a cause for resentment. It is indeed this capacity for witty speech, and plenty of it, that is the most noteworthy national characteristic, accounting for the country's eminence in playwrights, essayists and orators. This characteristic of the whole nation is strongly concentrated in the capital city, Dublin.

The political background is one of the striking things about Dublin of to-day, and has had to be treated at what may seem to some readers undue length. Other things must now be mentioned: things which strike the stranger almost from his first step on Dublin pavements. The Englishman used to the shopping centres of London or provincial towns will be shocked at the evidences of poverty in the midst of a great city. But this poverty, the almost proverbial lot of Ireland for centuries, is at any rate a little mitigated. Twenty years ago it was certainly worse; fifteen years ago, as bad and not yet redeemed by the promise of reform. For there are now several streets where extensive rehabilitation of Georgian houses is under way; terraces completely restored, with happy-looking families again at the windows, smile at the passer-by in all the glory of scrubbed brickwork and fresh coats of paint. There are also a number of modern housing schemes and other buildings (one especially in Harcourt Street)* which harmonize well with the old work without reproducing its features.

More than this, there has been another very great change since 1933; a change which has not only immeasurably improved Dublin, but has placed its amenities on a higher level than those of any other large city that I have visited. The biting criticism of Mr. Manning Robertson's *Cautionary Guide to Dublin* has done its work, and hoardings of unsightly advertisements have now disappeared from housefronts and empty sites. In one bound Dublin has ceased to be the most distressed of cities in its spoiled beauty, and takes pride of place as the capital of visible taste. Would that this shining example were followed by every city with a claim to civilization.

* The Four Provinces House, by Mr. Michael Scott.

22 THE ROTUNDA AND RUTLAND SQUARE. The Round Room was built 1764: John Ensor, architect

From a colour-print by S. F. Brocas, c. 1820

23   The Royal College of Surgeons, St. Stephen's Green, 1825–7
William Murray, architect

24   Steevens' Hospital, 1720–33

Dublin's poverty, shocking as it was and is, used to be partly compensated by the fact that Dublin was a centre of low prices. Everybody, from the nobility downwards, could live in Dublin for a fraction of the cost in contemporary London. Unfortunately this is now a thing of the past; food prices are for the most part actually higher than those in England. Until recently Eire was able to keep the burdens of its citizens light: they still enjoy relatively low taxation, and the worst features of the steady "wage-spiral" have hitherto been avoided; certain costs, notably transport, are very low indeed compared with those of other countries. But bread now costs about half as much again as in England; meat nearly twice as much; butter and cheese are scarce as well as expensive. It is not at all clear how the very poor are managing to exist at all, and many children look positively under-nourished. But though the wartime world shortage of food has made the situation worse, it must not be imagined that it created it.

The truly appalling state of the poor in Dublin in the eighteenth and early nineteenth centuries has been detailed in Professor Constantia Maxwell's authoritative book on *Dublin under the Georges*; all through that period conditions for the submerged had been terrible, but the most horrifying phase was still to come. This was the invasion by pauperdom of vast areas of what were once not merely respectable but almost palatial houses. Except for O'Connell (Sackville) Street and Parnell (Rutland) Square, practically the whole of the northern half of the eighteenth-century city is one enormous slum. The wide streets of noble brick and granite houses, absolutely unsurpassed as architecture and town-planning of their period, and the most notable historic survival to be found in a capital, are seen on closer inspection to house thousands of the great unwashed, living in inconceivable circumstances at the centre of the most exquisite capital of Europe.

The condition of these houses is amazing: magnificent panelled doors, patched and burst and drunkenly hanging awry; delicately proportioned fanlights now devoid of glass; smashed and never repaired panes and sashes in the windows; scaling paintwork; empty gaps and heaps of rubble that represent, not the fall of a land-mine, but some half-hearted attempt at slum-clearance. The contrast between the original

2*

11

DUBLIN

and present state of the northern streets harrows the observer;
entered with half-closed eyes, a street seems yet another gem,
result of good building, excellent design and taste, and enlightened town-planning; with eyes open, and nose alert, it
becomes a dishevelled and malodorous wreck. Yet even here
are indefatigable spirits, and not a street but shows some
brave window boxes of flowers at the second and third floors,
while larrikins lounge against the door-posts and children
scutter and squall below.

Nineteenth-century Ireland rid herself of the absentee
landlord and his rack-renting evictionist agent. Bad as many
of them doubtless were, one wonders if they can have excelled
the human sharks whose control of a great part of the capital
led to this ruin and desolation. It is to be hoped that the
work which is now beginning can be carried forward without
delay, for even the sturdiest of buildings cannot indefinitely
endure neglect and ill-treatment. It is imperative that all
that may be should be saved of this splendid inheritance. In
spite of everything, these Dublin streets are splendid, both as
specimens of historic architecture, and as the type of a civic
sense of responsibility. The Dublin Wide Street Commissioners, set up in 1757, were among the most remarkable
public bodies ever known, to judge from the success of their
work. There is probably no city in Europe, perhaps not in
the world, where sunlight and air, the bringers of health and
life, are so all-pervasive, so adequately brought home to
everybody. This cannot have been without its effect in
intensifying the lively and sparkling Dublin temperament.

As in all great cities, Dublin's population is maintained
and increased by immigration from the countryside. This
flow of people off the farms and on to the city streets is one
of the crying problems of Ireland, as of most European
countries. The limited opportunities and narrow "life" of the
farm and village no longer appeal to a generation brought up
on the wireless and the cinema. Ireland as a whole, and Dublin
in particular, is fond of the moving picture; perhaps because it
depicts a world so far removed from that of the normal
Irishman. The modern world seeks escape, and the highly
coloured melodrama of the screen forms an exquisite escape
for the simple and unsophisticated people of rural Eire.
There were Irish emigrants before ever there were films,
but how many of those who now leave Ireland are lured by the

12

25   Aerial view of central Dublin looking South down O'Connell Street—the Nelson Pillar in the centre

26   The Parnell Monument and Upper O'Connell Street from the Rotunda

27   College Green with the King William Statue, and the Bank of Ireland on the left, *c.* 1910

idea that both adventure and riches are waiting in New York or California?

Ireland is losing its agricultural background, and a large part of its people, and something radical must occur to change this trend, or national extinction will result. Not even Ireland can live off a tourist trade and one or two international airports. Just what is to be the remedy is not so clear. Some enthusiasts believe that if only the Irish spoke no English, they would be less likely to emigrate. This is true, but emigration depends on vital factors that go deeper than language. Thousands upon thousands of emigrants from Europe to the U.S.A., to South America and to the British colonies (I speak of the nineteenth century) were driven to this desperate course by actual famine, by terrible working conditions, and by hatred of conscription. The fact that they would have to learn a new language did not daunt these people, many of them in extreme poverty, and few of them highly educated. Besides, the Irish are naturally adventurous; Brendan may well have been the first European to reach America, and since then Irish missionaries and exiles have penetrated the whole world, blazing a trail of exploration, pioneering, revolutionary leadership and forlorn hopes.

When I referred to Dublin as an English-speaking capital, I may have surprised some innocents who imagine that the Irish of Dublin speak Gaelic as the Bohemians of Prague speak Czech. Not so; though most of the younger inhabitants have had to learn their language at school, even the fact that Irish is also the language of instruction in many schools has not made it a native tongue. Doubt is expressed whether it ever will become so—partly because the sudden forced expansion of the last twenty-five years has tended to corrupt the genuine language still spoken in the Gaeltacht. This is the small area in the west of Ireland where Irish is still spoken by a majority of the inhabitants. But the "pure" Gaelic area, where over 80 per cent *can* speak the language, is very restricted, and even there very few are unable to speak English. The fact that English is understood and normally spoken throughout Ireland, the rest of the British Isles, and in the U.S.A., Canada and Australia, where the emigrants mostly live, more than outweighs governmental legislation and propaganda.

By governmental adoption of certain Irish words and

phrases which are never translated, a nodding acquaintance with Gaelic is increasing, but outside the Gaeltacht it is only keen members of the Gaelic movement that actually converse in Irish. They are well hidden, for no-one ever seems to hear them at it in Dublin; the language of the shop and the street is universally English. The bilingualism of street- and station-nameplates is not the result of the political revolution, but of the efforts of the Gaelic League. The handbook issued for the British Association Meeting in Dublin in 1908 states that the street-names in Gaelic first appeared in 1898, and in ten years most of the Dublin area had been dealt with, and some railway stations were displaying Irish names.

The decline and revival of Irish is a tragi-comedy. It is sad that an historic language should die out, even though a truly universal language were to be the outcome. Until the nineteenth century Irish was the language of the peasantry, even close to Dublin. The building of military roads through the Dublin and Wicklow Mountains, and the "progressive" policy of English governments after the Union steadily drove it back. There is no need to attribute to the government any deliberate intention of destroying national sentiment. It was simply an accidental result of the "march of progress". But right up to the 'sixties and 'seventies Gaelic was the spoken language of the tenants on the estates of the Irish Middle West; George Moore, who was born in 1853, could remember monoglot Irishmen from the hills coming to pay their rent. Another generation passed before a few enthusiasts got together to revive the language, and by then it was too late. Irish was extinct in Leinster, and only in living use in remote districts; revival was bound to come out of books. That is where the difficulty still lies.

Irish, compared with English, is a difficult language: it has two grammatical genders, a complicated inflectional system, a principle of sound-changes (analogous to that in Welsh), and a cumbersome non-phonetic spelling. Apart from the unusually awkward spelling, the language is comparable to Latin, even more to Greek. This primitive state of development gives Irish its literary advantage; it has not been worn down by centuries of hard usage. But whereas the decay and corruption of English are due to centuries of use, there is (or so it is claimed) a very serious corruption of Irish by its sudden official transformation into a modern language. It is also a common criticism of the "Irish policy" that it has led to a lowering of the general standard of education. But an undue preponderance of Irish in the curriculum is inevitable—if the language is to be saved at all.

I am assuming that it is worth while that the language should be revived; and it seems that this assumption is warranted by the real literary contributions of the Gaeltacht during the last generation. The revival of English as a language of universal usage in the fourteenth century underlies all the features of lasting value in England's contribution to the world. After the trying period of transition, there is undoubtedly hope for Irish as the tongue of a great literature, which in two thousand years may rank with the work of Homeric and Periclean Greece, Julian and Augustan Rome, and Plantagenet and Tudor England. Historically there may be good ground for this hope, for Irish, which seems to have the requisites of a great language, has never yet been one. Not unless there is truth in the circumstantial evidence which would make the tongue of the Phoenician merchant-adventurers a form of Goidelic or "q.Celtic" closely akin to Ulster Gaelic and Highland Erse. Whether it is true that a Scottish Highland missionary found himself able to converse with an obscure tribe in the Atlas Mountains, and whether the few known fragments of Punic are correctly paralleled by modern Gaelic, I do not know; what is certain is that if Punic had a great literature, it has perished. So the way is clear for modern Irish, and if it can make good as the medium of a fresher, less jaded epoch, let us wish it well.

For the present at any rate Dublin is a city of the English language, and this is eminently suitable to the mediator between London and New York. To a Londoner at least, what an amazing city Dublin is! To an Englishman Dublin has the virtues of a foreign capital without the drawbacks: artificial animosities have not annulled the kinship which has grown up through centuries of intermarriage between the peoples of the British Isles. Dublin seems to foreshadow the qualities of a new type of supra-national city; let us have a look at her.

II
Dublin Now

NATIONALISM IS NONSENSE; BUT IT CAN HAVE INDIRECT results which do make sense. So far as Dublin is now both a flourishing and a promising city, it is the outcome of nationalism, building on the remains of an alien aristocratic tradition. I say alien with some hesitation, for the great Ascendancy culture of the seventeenth and eighteenth centuries had a quality and a spirit quite unlike that of Georgian England. It had, and through its buildings and its books still promulgates, an atmosphere characteristically Irish. In ancient Ireland itself the ruling and educated class of different epochs represented a thin cream, result of invasion or inbreeding by certain stocks. There always will be a ruling minority of some kind everywhere, distinct from the great body of peasants or industrial workers.

This is not to say that a national sympathy cannot be established between the components of what we loosely term a nation. To take an obvious example, a high degree of sympathy and unity of purpose on the part of English men and women of both sexes and all types is reflected in Chaucer's *Prologue* and pilgrimage episodes; the plays of Shakespeare and even of the learned Ben Jonson could tickle the ribs of the groundlings as well as the palates of the more sophisticated. The wildly unexpected success of the two great dramatic ventures of modern Ireland, the Abbey (**28**) and Gate Theatres, has proved the possibility of re-creating under modern conditions a great deal of this national sympathy and unity, without excluding by mere chauvinism the supreme values of international art on its highest level. Ireland came perilously near this last catastrophe; it looked for a time as though there was to be a permanent cleavage between "patriotic" and highly insular support of the Irish language, peasant art, Romanesque Revival and extreme Roman Catholicism on the one hand; and the English language, international culture, the Georgian and modern movements, Protestantism and liberal thought on the other.

29 The Irish House

28 The Abbey

THE SPIRIT OF DUBLIN

30   The Corn Exchange, Burgh Quay, and the Custom House
From a colour-print by S. F. Brocas, 1820

I believe that I am not premature in saying that the crisis is now past: the uncommon sense of the Irish, and particularly of Dubliners, and six years of recent national emergency have saved the situation. Fifteen and even ten years ago it looked as though Eire was so disgusted (officially) with the Georgian remains of the Ascendancy that it was determined to sweep them away to build a peasant-Gaelic capital in their place; to root out for ever, so soon as practical considerations would permit, every memory of a culture which it had taken three-quarters of a millenium to build. Uncommon sense has prevailed, or at least is prevailing; the centuries of so-called English Rule are seen to have produced great and lasting values which can be incorporated in the Irish tradition, and it is no longer necessary to jettison all the world-famous Irish names in order to display the better an unpronounceable array of Gaelic heroes.

This is not an English sneer: I am willing, indeed anxious, to learn to pronounce these names of beings who have meant so much, not only to Ireland, but to European civilization as a whole. But it happens to be true that the world can far more readily accept the greatness of Homer, Virgil, Dante, Chaucer, Villon, Shakespeare, Swift, Burke, Tolstoy, Shaw, than it can for example Mickiewicz or Cervantes or Llywelyn ap Ifan ap y Gof. Mr. Denis Gwynn in his *Edward Martyn and the Irish Revival* tells, very much to the point, the story of Standish O'Grady, who knew no Irish himself, but produced very fine English versions of *Cuchulain* and other Gaelic sagas. Meeting Patrick Pearse, O'Grady pronounced the hero's name as Cutch-ul-ane, whereon Pearse corrected him, explaining that the correct pronunciation was Coo-hu-lin. "O'Grady was overwhelmed by the discovery, and after a long pause informed Pearse that he would have written an entirely different book if he had known the correct sound of the name."

There is no getting away from the fact that the majority of the really distinguished members of the Irish revival belonged to the "hated" Protestant Ascendancy: the Yeats family, J. M. Synge; George Russell (110), Dr. Douglas Hyde, and Lady Gregory; while outside this group are the universal names of Oscar Wilde and Mr. George Bernard Shaw. George Moore, though bred up a Catholic, found that his own temperament and a considerable period of his family tradition

17

were Protestant, and the movement thankfully accepted the help even of Lionel Johnson, the most distinguished English poet of his time, who was Catholic only by conversion, and invented a largely mythical set of Irish ancestors to soothe his friends' susceptibilities or merely to satisfy his own sense of fitness. I am not trying to disparage the work done by the "pure" Irish in other directions, but simply to emphasize the impossibility of ignoring the ascendancy in any survey or assessment of Irish culture.

Taking the whole of Irish history as known to us, it is certain that important, indeed vital contributions have been made by Pagans, Christians, Catholics, Protestants, Freethinkers; by Iberians, Gaels and other early immigrants, and the later invaders, Danes, Normans and English; by princes, priests, peasants and people of all sorts and conditions. There is not now (and never has been) such a scientifically distinguishable person as an Irishman; but the people of Ireland do tend to have in common a number of important characteristics which may or may not be present in a given individual. There is an Irish eye, an Irish walk, notably an Irish mouth—source of wit and eloquence; and though types are many and varied, the practised eye soon learns to pick them out by some quality which they share. If there is a diversity of types in Ireland as a whole, still more so is this true of Dublin, which has been an important harbour for at least two thousand years; under foreign control for practically the whole of the period, over half that time, in which it has been admittedly Ireland's chief city.

Now, seat of an Irish government for only a quarter of a century, Dublin already shows signs of becoming a real centre of national unity, as well as the cultural phenomenon she has been for several hundred years already. The assertion of that uncommon sense to which I have before referred, sees to it that the old rancours are, so far as is humanly possible, buried. The election in 1938 of Dr. Douglas Hyde as first President of Eire did not merely crown the life-work of a poet who abandoned literary ambition to revive the national language, but demonstrated that Catholic Ireland was proud to have a Protestant Anglo-Norman as its official head. And possibly a wider gesture of generosity, the Honorary Freedom of the City of Dublin was conferred on Mr. George Bernard Shaw on the 26th July 1946. Sharply contrasting with the

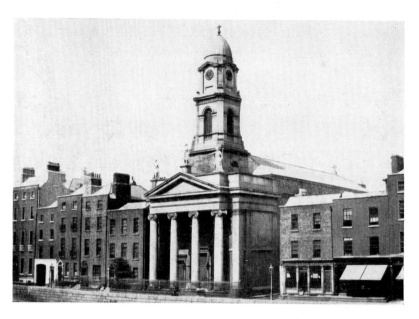

31   St. Paul's Catholic Church, Arran Quay, 1835-7

32   St. Andrew's Catholic Church, Westland Row, 1832-4

34 Powerscourt House, William Street, 1771–4
Robert Mack, architect

33 Municipal Buildings, formerly Newcomen's
Bank, 1781
Thomas Ivory, architect

policy of minority-baiting and spite indulged in by a number
of the continental successor-states in the period 1920–40,
Eire has preserved an unbroken continuity in her administration and departmental work, in the functions of her cultural,
learned, and professional bodies, and in her art. This republic
is still adorned by many Royal academies and institutions of
standing; the Protestant Church of Ireland still remains in
possession of the two mediaeval cathedrals and of the ancient
parish churches; Ulster King of Arms has been gracefully
replaced, with continuity of personnel, traditions and equipment, by a Genealogical Officer, whose heraldic and other
services are in far greater demand than were those of his
predecessors under the old order. In the unique Heraldic
Museum in Dublin Castle, formed by Ulster King of Arms,
and in process of augmentation by the new owners, are the
strange precedents for the appointment of a Herald by
a republican government: the patents of the seventeenth-
century ex-King of Arms, Richard Carney, granted by Oliver
and Richard Cromwell—appointments which refer in cold and
unheraldic English to the "bloody and rebellious Irish".
All these things are happy auguries, and signs that the price-
less possession of a sense of humour has not been thrown
away by patriotic fanaticism.

History is determined by two main series of causes falling
under the heads of heredity and environment. The potential
response of an individual to cultural stimulus lies in his
hereditary make-up; but his actual output is determined very
largely by environment. On inspection, it is evident that the
particular qualities of the civilization of Dublin cannot be
mainly racial: the past and present physical types and their
psychological counterparts are too diverse for that. So we
are left with the forces of environment as the factors which
account for Dublin as a phenomenon. But we can define still
further. Environment itself may be human, artificial; or
natural and geophysical. Among the most important artificial factors are religion and social status; and it is clear that
no one sect, neither any one class, has exclusive or even chief
responsibility for the culture of Dublin. If Protestantism can
claim a majority of the outstanding figures of world-wide
reputation, Catholicism has a more than negligible minority,
and almost a monopoly of the human background, while a
Paganism far deeper than either sect provides the whole of

the national mythology as well as the local folk-lore. No stratum of society provides the springboard for a clear majority of the great figures.

It looks as though the decisive causes of Dublin's greatness in the realms of culture and human achievement lie as much or nearly as much in geology, topography and climate, as the very existence of Dublin depends on the River Liffey.

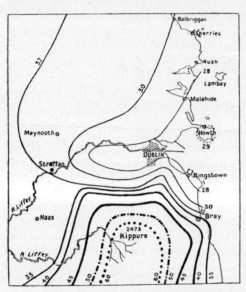

35 Rainfall gradient (in inches) of the Dublin region

The precise sphere of work of each man of genius whose career has adorned the city doubtless has depended upon his personal heredity and family circumstances; but I believe that the source of attraction which has connected so many such men with this small area must lie mainly in its physical situation, and in the natural forces which determine its destiny. It is self-evident that a great centre of population must stand upon a river or other adequate supply of fresh water, and as a riverine settlement Dublin can be grouped with Vienna, with Paris, and with London. Its river is, all the same, much the smallest of the four; only since the building of canals has Dublin had any effective water-transport to its back lands. Like London, and unlike its continental rivals, Dublin lies close to the sea, and large sea-going vessels penetrate almost to its centre. Whereas London's intellectual quarters have steadily retreated from the sea since the days of Chaucer, Dublin's O'Connell Bridge is almost within a stone's throw of the masts and spars of shipping (30). And the queer thing is, that while London has moved westward; Dublin marches eastwards, towards the open water (1). This unusual pro-

36   A Cross-Channel steamer at the North Wall

37   Dublin exports: Guinness's stout and Jacob's biscuits

38 Opening of the Dublin & Kingstown Railway
From a print of 1834

39 View from the Foster Aqueduct at Broadstone
From a print by W. M. Craig, 1816

cedure has been at the rate of about one mile in the last five hundred years, but it seems hardly possible for it to continue further.

Dublin's position, and the conformation of the surrounding country, give rise to another peculiarity: in an excessively damp country prone to a rainfall of even 60 or 80 inches, Dublin alone enjoys less than 28 inches on the average, and a very small wedge of surrounding country, from Balbriggan on the north to Killiney on the south, is the only part of the whole country with less than 30 inches (35). At the same time, Dublin's July temperature of some 60° is about the maximum for the country, and the frequency of *warm* East winds from the sea gives the city and its immediate neighbourhood an exceptionally high number of hours of sunshine. The winter climate is relatively mild and many Mediterranean plants will grow around Dublin, which cannot stand the open air even in southern England, 200 miles nearer the equator. This last point is not a mere artificial distinction concerning only cultivated plants: the immediate surroundings of Dublin have a remarkable natural flora and fauna of the type known as "Lusitanian"—an earth-worm, several spiders and wood-lice, a millipede, are either peculiar to Dublin, or are hardly known elsewhere within the British Isles. Certain species also occur in the Pyrenees, while the Dublin House-Spider, unknown outside Ireland, has a Pyrenean spider for its nearest relation. There are also species from an ancient northern and arctic zone of distribution. Nature and art have conspired to make Dublin unique.

The contribution made by art is linked to a history of strange and varied episodes. Dublin is unlike London (for example) largely for historical reasons, and these are themselves the product of its situation. Until about two thousand years ago the site of Dublin and the site of London had a great deal in common. No city of importance stood at either place, but in both cases significance attached to an estuary accessible to sea-going vessels, forded by a north-south route. Both sites faced the east; both were inhabited by peoples of Iberian stock, going back to neolithic times, overlaid with Bronze Age invaders, and again by workers of iron from continental Gaul. In both cases the language of the inhabitants was Celtic. And then something happened to the site of London: it was occupied by the military forces of Rome, and a walled, town-planned colonial city erected to dominate a rearranged transport system for all southern Britain.

London was laid out for the Roman legionary, and even to-day London's civilization (which is that exported to the Commonwealth and the world) bears the stamp of the successful engineer. All the diversity of western and mediterranean Europe cannot conceal a certain common factor learnt from old Rome—a preoccupation with the show-front of material fitness and organization. The legacy of Rome makes it difficult for men to forget the "duties" of housing, hygiene, communications and public responsibility. England, which benefited by a strong infusion of the unregimented Saxons, Angles, Danes and Normans, suffers less in some respects than does France. But leave the realm of Rome in any direction, and a new easy-going outlook is felt. It is well known that in the Scandinavian countries the King can go about unattended with perfect safety—law and order exist without squads of plain-clothes men. In Ireland, in spite of its history of rebellion and riot, we see another facet of the same truth—no western country is so unaffected by officialdom. The police-state, that menace which threatens human sanity, is the longest-living and the most sinister symptom of Roman domination—I do not of course refer to the Roman Catholic Church. For any country which is resistant to this creeping cancer, the rest of the world may be profoundly thankful.

So the first and greatest of factors which have made Dublin so different is its exemption from Roman dominion. Then again, though Dublin as a city almost owes its existence, certainly its importance, to the Dane and Norseman, it escaped the predominance of Angle and Saxon who form the stolid and unimaginative core of southern England. The influx of "Saxons" from England between the twelfth and nineteenth centuries comprised for the most part adventurous traders and skilled artists and craftsmen, obviously untypical of the English population. The very fact that Dublin during those centuries was a frontier city kept it free from the humdrum and unenterprising exponents of normality. Contact, even hostile contact, with types as diverse as the Gaelic, the Iberian and the Norse are from the Saxon, and interbreeding over a period of centuries have seen to it that the Dubliner of to-day, even when not noticeably witty, has a welcome quality of the unexpected.

Considering the poverty of many of its citizens, Dublin is a remarkably healthy city, yet hygiene has not become the overworked fetish that it so often is in the modern world. There are still people who refer, quite seriously, to "dear dirty Dublin", but the pervasive sunlight in the wide streets, the whiffs of sea breeze, and the sight of the mountains, all help to create a feeling that it is good clean dirt. One of the less pleasant results is the lack of care taken over the behaviour of dogs, but where else could one find so pleasing a notice as this, from a shop in Dalkey, the old Norse port of Dublin and southern limit of the Pale:

HOURS OF BUSINESS
10.30 a.m. to 1 p.m.   2.30 p.m. to 8 p.m.
Half-Day Wednesday
Never open for Dogs

The uncommon sense of Dublin I have already mentioned; a striking example occurs in the announcement that American maternity hospitals have just "discovered" that it may be psychologically unsound to separate new-born infants from their mothers, as well as unnecessary on hygienic grounds. But the Rotunda Lying-In Hospital (**22, 130**) of Dublin has for years, since it took steps to prevent children being overlain by their mothers, slung the cradles on the feet of the mothers' beds. And the Rotunda is still, as it has almost always been through its two centuries of life, the healthiest of its kind. Dr. O'Donel Browne in his recent history quotes the comparative figures of a hundred years ago for maternal mortality: between 1829 and 1849 in Paris 4·18 per cent of mothers died; in Vienna 5·35 per cent; at the Rotunda 1·34 per cent. Besides this, the Rotunda has always advocated the sensible and "old-fashioned" course of mothers having children in their own homes wherever possible. The dehumanized world of to-day can learn a lot from Dublin.

Freedom from unneeded formality is carried to considerable lengths: anyone who has made application for a Reader's Ticket at the British Museum will appreciate the methods of the National Library of Ireland (**48**). "Sure, the librarian that issues tickets is away just now, but the thing for you to do is to go ahead as if you had a ticket already." The total stranger in museum or gallery may be pressed by an attendant in the most friendly manner to send up his name to the curator, who "would be sorry to miss a visitor". It is not fable but fact that people of all classes in Dublin are glad to find time for casual conversation, maybe begun with a personal remark, but often helpful and seldom boring. In general, there is a pleasant atmosphere that rules and regulations are made to be broken at convenience, or if not, that as in Toytown offenders will "have their names and addresses took". Even the regulations that do exist are not burdensome: the prohibited hour of 2.30 to 3.30 p.m., during which the pubs are shut, hardly allows the barman a short nap, but is unutterably welcome on summer afternoons to the thirsty wayfarer inured to the long drought enforced in England.

At the present time there are several favourite topics of discussion. Political issues are naturally among them, and the chief of these is the government's enforcement of the Irish language upon the whole state educational system; an enforcement regarded by the average Dubliner (an English speaker born and bred) as an unfair handicap. Linked to this is the policy of ploughing up the grazing counties, notably Co. Meath, for the benefit of transported Irish-speakers from the Gaelic West. The censorship of books and films is another hardy perpetual; for in spite of the protests of W. B. Yeats (109) and his literary supporters, modern Eire suffers from an extremely thin-skinned moral censorship. Fortunately there is no political ban, but the definition of what is capable of giving offence to morals and religion is so wide that the banning of books and cutting of films reaches a humorously fantastic point.

The keen interest in general issues forms a real body of public opinion on matters where governmental bureaucracy presses too far. In more than one instance the Eire Supreme Court has ruled that legislation is unconstitutional and therefore void. This cannot happen in England, unless a very monstrous loophole has been left by careless drafting, for England has no written Constitution. But Eire at present enjoys the benefit of a fundamental document which actually does guarantee a high degree of freedom of action to individuals and to minorities. Thus if a man wants to avoid having his children taught Irish, he can send them to be educated privately if he has the money to pay, and they can go on to Trinity College without passing the Irish tests essential

40   St. George's Church from Eccles Street

41   Hardwicke Street, and St. George's Church, 1802–13
Francis Johnston, architect

42 Doorways in Merrion Square, *c.* 1790

43 Doorway in Ely Place, 1770, with contemporary ironwork

at the National University. Furthermore, public opinion
has to some extent modified the undue favouring of Catholic
Nationalists which followed the setting up of the Free State.
Some swing of the pendulum was doubtless inevitable, and
though it is still necessary for many Protestant Irishmen of education to seek careers in England or elsewhere, they themselves
admit that the home position is gradually improving and that
mere bigotry is on the wane. In Dublin such discrimination,
in either sense, always has been milder than elsewhere, and
never comparable with the extremism of Belfast and the north.

Other types of public opinion are fostered by the large
number of exhibitions and cultural events, and by the
theatres, to say nothing of the musical renown of the choirs of
St. Patrick's Cathedral and of the Catholic Pro-Cathedral.
Art exhibitions are thronged by a much wider variety of
human types than their counterparts in London, and there is
a good deal of artistic discussion. As to the theatre, the world
fame of the Abbey (28) does not outrun its popularity with
its own patrons, and packed houses are the rule. One excellent
custom of the Abbey, is that members of the audience not in
their seats at the rise of the curtain are firmly excluded until the
end of the act. This has several salutary effects: it enormously
improves the enjoyment of the audience; helps to maintain the
actors' high standard of performance, which can be so marred
by interruptions; and creates a psychological discipline favour-
able not merely to punctuality, but to attendance as such.

An outstanding feature of Dublin life to-day is the absence
of "high society"; since the abolition of the office of Governor-
General, the last flickering semblance of the old social leadership of the Castle has disappeared, and though the President
appears in ceremonial garb on formal occasions, Mr. De
Valera's party have steadily set their faces against the implications of the top hat and the starched shirt. Recalling the
fantastic lengths to which the worship of these symbols of
civilization has been carried in the new Turkey, one can but
feel that the founders of free Ireland are wise in their generation. In due course a genuine society based on real values may
and should arise; meanwhile it is refreshing to find a discreet
avoidance of the sham which has been foisted upon the world
since the French Revolution. For the present there is an
almost total absence of that cream of well-dressed men and
women such as form a noteworthy feature of London. But

even in its palmy days, Dublin was less artificial in its distinctions than London: the great Sheridan's father was an actor-manager, but his grandfather was a clergyman and the intimate friend of Dean Swift.

There is something of this approach to a classless society in the theatres, with their amazingly low-priced seats—stalls at four shillings; even more so in restaurants. There is only one in Dublin of international standing, Jammet's, a relic of the opening of the century and product of French enterprise. Otherwise there is no great gulf in price or in quality of food in the series of eating houses which stretches from the discreet civil service quarter around Merrion Row, down through the crowded shops of Grafton Street and Westmoreland Street, and across the Liffey to the Nelson Pillar (**44**), and even to the smaller cafés around Abbey Street, combinations of the chop-house and the good-pull-up-for-carmen. Recently there has been a much-discussed rise in most prices due to demands for higher pay in the catering trade; this has added an unduly burdensome item to the budgets of the business men and women who have to find their lunch in town. The increased prices are based on the influx of English and other tourists ready to pay for unrationed food, and it is clear that some form of price-control here, as in other directions is badly needed.*

But in another direction Dublin is provided with a greater nicety of social distinction than London: the suburban trains still contain first-class carriages, much patronized, and the Great Northern line, alone in the British Isles, retains second class as well. In the early days of Ireland's first railroad, from Westland Row to Kingstown, there were even four classes, though no exact description of the fourth degree of discomfort and dirt seems to have been preserved. In many ways the history of Irish railways is an interesting one: the Kingstown line is said to have been the first in the world to introduce workmen's tickets, and for many years from its opening (**38**), its trains ran every half-hour throughout the day, with extras at the hours of peak traffic. Gradually the growth of private motor transport, and the electric tram as far as Dalkey, which runs every few minutes, have reduced the service, but there are still, in spite of fuel shortage, twenty-eight daily trains in each direction between Dublin and Dun Laoghaire,

* The autumn of 1947 saw the introduction of such controls.

44   The Nelson Pillar, 1808. William Wilkins, architect

45 The General Post Office, 1815-20, by Francis Johnston, and the Nelson Pillar, 1808, by William Wilkins

From the water-colour by S. F. Brocas, 1818

from 7 a.m. to 11 p.m. When the extension from Kingstown to Dalkey was opened in July 1844, nearly ten years after the line to Kingstown, it was worked on the atmospheric principle, with stationary pumping engines and a piston working in a large iron tube closed along an upper slit with flaps of greased leather. Like the similar line in South Devon, it worked phenomenally well at first, but soon became out of order and had to be replaced by the despised steam locomotives of its rivals.

The early railways in Ireland were even more diverse in their gauges than those of England, and instead of the straightforward struggle between Stephenson's standard and Brunel's seven-foot broad-gauge, the little island was threatened with a complexity as bad as that which still hinders transport in the continents of Australia and South America. It can be claimed as one of the good deeds of the English in Ireland that the Inspector-General of Railways resolved the problem by adding the various existing gauges together, and dividing by their number. The result was 5 feet 3 inches, which was made the legal gauge for all future lines; those already built were converted to it. Although there now seems something slightly comic about this method of averages, the outcome was eminently satisfactory, and it is a great misfortune that the Irish gauge did not become that of the world. With its adequate gauge, and wide-spreading central plain, Ireland might be a country of railway records, but the volume of traffic has never warranted the cost and fuel-expenditure required for high speeds, and Irish trains, even before the recent war, were among the slowest, though the most comfortable, of Western Europe. Now a great controversy is raging between the transport monopoly, C.I.E., and the general public, as to the existence of branch lines. C.I.E. make out quite a good economic case for transferring all short-distance and most medium-distance traffic to the road, and their policy is based on the reports of planning experts made over the last twenty years. But it is not clear that the enormous development of the road system is justified, or that it is wise for so small a country as Ireland to make itself dependent upon imported oil. What is certain is that for the present the bus services substituted for the branch lines are grossly inadequate, and combined with the coal-starved rail services represent a very marked regression from the admirably

developed transport of thirty to forty years ago, when the
Balfour scheme of locally subsidized light railways was in its
prime.

Not only the railway, but the tram services, are in a state
of eclipse. Gradually the whole elaborate network of Dublin
tramways is being abolished in favour of petrol buses which
have some real advantages, and others more illusory. Dublin
used to claim, with a good deal of truth, that it had the finest
tramway system in the world (**46**). Its drawbacks were and
are: overhead cables, rails, noise. As against this, the service
is reasonably safe and sure, fairly fast, devoid of fumes and
smell, and more elastic in carrying capacity than are the
substituted buses, which besides cannot carry bicycles and
small perambulators. This last advantage of the tram, in
a city which swarms with children, was a very great one. But
a good many years ago now the fiat went forth: the tram is
obsolete, and must be cleared from the world's streets. Un-
wieldy and obstructive as it is, the tram has a sort of half-
personality which I, for one, regret in its passing. As the
camel to the desert, so the tram is the true ship of the suburb.
O well remembered trams with open upper decks, you that
ran through London's Highgate and Finchley to the verge of
Hadley Woods; that linked the Nelson Pillar with the Bay and
Howth, with Chapelizod and Lucan, with woody Rathfarnham,
you are gone, to return no more. So while they enjoy a brief
reprieve, let us career through cobbled streets with the No. 8,
that last and noblest route, through Merrion Square, past the
Horse Show Grounds at Ballsbridge, near the shores of the
majestic Bay by Booterstown and Blackrock, through the long
narrow street of erstwhile Kingstown, halting at passing loops,
and out and up through countrified Bullock to the ancient
heights of Dalkey. Lovers of the road voyage through the dusk,
of the lighted argosy of midnight return, make haste to take
your tickets. After so many thousand journeys, few remain.

Yes, Dublin transport to-day is not what it was. The
transition to the planned schemes of modern economy fell
foul of a world war, here known as "the emergency", and
the result has been unfortunate. In little over fifty years
Dublin has increased in population from under 250,000 to
over 500,000—the 1946 Census shows that the County
Borough has for the first time passed the half-million. But
whereas in 1893 there were over 2,000 horse-drawn vehicles,

cabs and outside cars, for hire, and between 200 and 300 tram-cars, in 1944 there were less than 700 public hire vehicles (223 Motor Taxis, 219 Motors for Private Hire, 236 Horse-drawn Cars and Cabs), 95 trams, and 496 buses. The increase in the number of buses has to be offset, not only by the reduction in trams, but also by the complete withdrawal of the western railway services to stations within a thirty-mile radius, and serious reduction of the remaining services. In

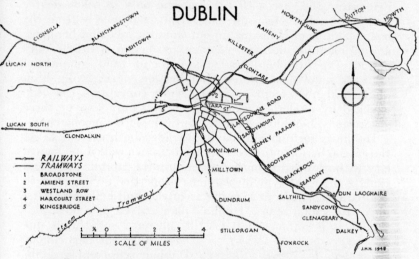

46 Dublin's suburban transport at its height. The steam tramway to Blessington and Poulaphouca has gone; the electric trams are going; the stations on the main lines to the West have been closed

1941 horse-drawn vehicles had reached their nadir (only 81 licensed in Dublin), but the restrictions on petrol and private motoring brought about an increase during the rest of the war period. The end of the war has put a flood of motors back on the roads, and the cars and cabs are once again dwindling away; but the fact that they still linger at all puts the final touch to that magnificent background of Dublin Life—the Georgian streets (**40, 41, 99, 100**).

For there are two fundamental things underlying the Dublin of the present—the one lasting, as if eternal; the other constantly changing, never static, always being pulled down, built up. For countless centuries there have been the bay, the river, the mountains; for less than two, almost all of the man-made city, the quays, the bridges, the streets, the churches, the public buildings. Dublin's contribution to the world, her wit, intellectual brilliance, temperament, are a many-faceted jewel. Her streets are that jewel's setting. And because, unlike most great cities, she has been able to preserve most of the setting contrived by the greatest period in her past existence, Dublin speaks with one voice. Her appeal is integrated, not out of tune with itself, as is so deplorably the case with London, and only to a less degree with Paris. Paris has suffered terribly, not merely from the over-planning of Haussmann, but from the fact that her great age of planning and development coincided with the only period of positively degraded architecture and commercial art ever known in France. London has never really been planned at all, except by Nash, whose conception has been wrecked by modern commercialism after only two or three generations; London is majestic, but completely incoherent.

Dublin is fortunate in having avoided both extremes. At the crucial period in her development from a walled mediaeval city with crowded suburbs into a cultural capital, she found exactly the right type of planners; propertied noblemen with exalted ideas, and enterprising architects and building crafts-men with sound sense. Dublin's plan arrived piecemeal, but though it is unfinished it is still coherent, and this is due basically to the particularly Dubliner sense and sensibili-ty, as well as to the enlight-ened continuity provided by the Wide Streets Commis-sion, founded in 1757. The greatest of all Dublin's archi-tectural secrets is her uncan-ny skill in the combination of the curve with the straight line in flowing patterns, avoiding monotony as well as fantasy (47). To this we owe the eloquent grace, the rhythm, and the unfailing variety which we find in the view of Dublin.

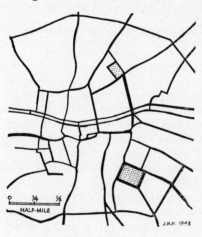

47 The Dublin pattern of streets

30

48 The National Library of Ireland, 1884
Sir Thomas N. Deane and Sir Thomas M. Deane, architects

49 The National Gallery of Ireland, 1859-64
Francis Fowke, architect; portico and additions by Sir Thomas
N. Deane

50   The Custom House, 1781-91
James Gandon, architect

III
The View of Dublin

IT IS A CENTURY-AND-A-HALF SINCE JAMES MALTON RECORDED the triumphs of Dublin's classic age in his *Picturesque and Descriptive View*, published between 1792 and 1799. He was just in time; ten years later the Union had killed the metropolitan spirit which had been fostered by the independent Parliament of Grattan. Ten years earlier would have been too early to display James Gandon's three great contributions to architecture; the Custom House (1781–91) (**50**); the Corinthian eastern front of the Parliament House (1785) (**71, 72**); and the Four Courts (1786–96) (**53, 60**). All the same, some really important additions have been made to the city since the Union. Chief of these, and going back only to 1880, is the building of the new O'Connell Bridge on the site of Carlisle Bridge (**144**). The significance of the new bridge is in its width, equal to the full expanse of O'Connell Street, and giving ample space to the streams of traffic which pour southwards into D'Olier and Westmoreland Streets. No bridge in London has equivalent dignity or impressiveness, for the greater width of the Thames and its importance as a waterway forbid any comparable design.

Architecturally, the General Post Office (**45**) of 1815, designed by the eclectic Francis Johnston, and the Nelson Pillar (**44**) of 1808, by William Wilkins of Norwich, represent the afterglow of Dublin's classic age, as does also Johnston's earlier work, St. George's Church (1802–13) in Hardwicke Place (**40, 41**). The Nelson Pillar is a grand work, without which the long stretch of O'Connell Street would lose much of its vitality. Fatuous suggestions for its removal have come from traffic maniacs who, apart from their total disregard for aesthetics, fail to visualize the chaos which would result from creating a through current of cross-town traffic at this point. In fact, the slight obstruction presented by the base of the Pillar to the main streams of North-South road-users serves as a most valuable warning.

The Pillar has been termed "Dublin's Glory" for no apparent

reason; for though it is certainly a notable sight, it can hardly
compare with several of the greater buildings of the city in
architectonic importance. But it is both a convenient and
intrinsically valuable focal point, from which radiates the
transport system. O'Connell Street is the only street in the
inner city which runs for a considerable distance in an
absolutely straight line; it is redeemed from the soulless
frigidity of gridiron planning by its great width, one hundred
and fifty feet, and by the Nelson Pillar at its centre. All the
other great thoroughfares of Dublin have their own persónal-
ities, diversified with squares, churches, public buildings, or
merely by their gentle curves and changes of direction. At
the same time, the general plan of Dublin is an easy one to
grasp, and represents in all its phases the historic development of one basic theme; the lowest crossing of a tidal river
by a great road. The main crossing has moved downstream
nearly three-quarters of a mile within the period of recorded
history, but the building of new bridges has simply empha-
sized the basic form of the city which has grown from this
nucleus. At present the vital centre lies at O'Connell Bridge:
across the city runs the River Liffey, accessible to large
ships only a few hundred yards to the east; linking the two
halves is a main land-artery, from the Drumcondra Road on
the north, through Parnell Square and O'Connell Street to
Grafton Street and St. Stephen's Green to the south. Look at
the map, and then, standing on the Bridge, the main frame-
work will become plain.

Down river is the splendid bulk of the Custom House (**50**)
obscured by the Loop Line railway viaduct of 1891. Probably
more controversy has raged over this viaduct than over any
other single problem of Dublin planning. It is not merely a
point of local interest, for there are wider implications. The
Irish railways before the Loop Line was built were cut in
half by the Liffey: there was no through connexion at all
between the Kingstown line and any of the main trunk routes
to the north, west, and south. By means of less than one mile
of elevated track, the main difficulty was solved, and there is
no doubt of the functional utility of this little City of Dublin
Junction Railway. But to leave the port accessible by water,
the bridge had to be upstream of the Custom House, and the
great view was cut in half by lattice girders. Of course the
ideal solution would be a tunnel, following the same line on

51 Looking down the quays, with O'Donovan Rossa (Richmond) Bridge in the foreground

52 Looking up the quays to the dome of the Four Courts

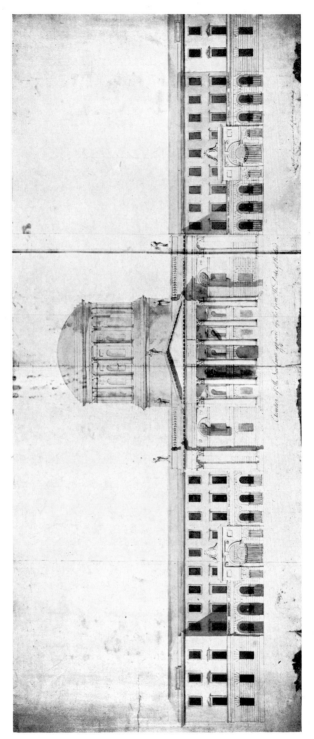

53 James Gandon's approved elevation for the Four Courts, 1785

plan, with low-level stations beneath the present Westland
Row and Amiens Street; but the cost has always been regarded
as absolutely prohibitive. So long as railways last, the loop
will be needed, and needed where it is now; if the aesthetes are
sincere, they will collect at least half the cost of making a
tunnel, and worry the powers that be until the job is done.

It is still possible to get fine views of the Custom House;
one of the best is from under the viaduct itself, by the entrance
to Tara Street Station. This view is indeed so good as to be
worth arranging as a surprise. Send on your heavy baggage,
leave the boat at Kingstown Pier, walk to the station, and take
the next Dublin train to Tara Street: the port of Dublin in
the limpid morning light will well repay a little extra trouble.
The other good view is from a little distance eastward, along
the southern quays. Turning seaward, the channel runs out
in a stately curve along the South Wall, steadily broadening
until the water of the open Bay is reached between the Poolbeg
and North Bull Lighthouses. From the Custom House to the
Poolbeg Light is over four miles in a straight line, and the
walk through Ringsend is even longer. But if a bicycle can
be had, this is one of the best of Dublin excursions. Setting
off down Pearse Street (Great Brunswick Street aforetime) the
Grand Canal Dock, generally inhabited by one or two small
coasting schooners, is crossed, and the squalid little village
of Ringsend entered. Once the dreary point of entry for the
English traveller, Ringsend now presents nothing of interest,
and the next mile of the wall is fringed on its south side by
rows of little cottage-tenements, and towards the deep-water
channel by the main sewage outfall works. Then come the
remains of the old Pigeon House Fort, once a packet station
before the days of Howth and Kingstown harbours, now given
over to a great electricity works whose chimneys can be seen
smoking from the far coasts of the Bay. For nearly two miles
beyond the Pigeon House the wall stretches, right out to the
centre of the Bay, at low tide fringed on the south by the South
Bull sand, but at high tide a mere dividing line between two
great expanses of water. There is very nearly the illusion of
being marooned on some forgotten island, perpetually kept at
its distance by Dublin, Dun Laoghaire, and the crouching
Gibraltar of Howth.

On a summer morning the view from the Poolbeg Lighthouse is enchanting; two miles off are the wooded slopes

of Clontarf and Raheny, and in between the golf links on the North Bull; but otherwise there is a vast surrounding expanse of water, shimmering in the sunlight and only broken by the distant sails of fishing smacks or yachts off Kingstown Harbour, or the occasional wake of a steamer entering or leaving the port. But you may, as I did, find the silence shattered by a weird chorus of titans, reminiscent at the same time of a Russian cathedral service and a chantey, now fading away and then rising to an eldritch shriek. It is one of the Ballast Board's dredgers at work, keeping the seaway clear.

Now that the dangers of a lee shore have been removed by steam-power, it is hard to realize the appalling dangers of such a roadstead as Dublin Bay before the walls were built. On account of the sands, vessels were not able to enter the port in safety except by broad daylight in calm weather, until in 1717 a line of wooden piling was carried along from Ringsend to the site of the Pigeon House. The stone walls carrying a broad roadway were begun in 1748 and finished to the Pigeon House in less than seven years. The end of the wall, at first marked by a floating light and a wooden house, got its name from the first caretaker, Pidgeon, who was a man of enterprise and made the remote breakwater a place of resort and his storehouse a popular hostel. Later on this became a packet station with a permanent hotel, only to be superseded by Howth in 1813, when the Government bought the buildings and extended them into a strongly fortified post. There is a general belief that its purpose was oppressive: the Pidgeonhouse Fort was to be a safe bridgehead for a British landing force, or a refuge for the administration in case of rebellion. But it never had any part to play in the changes of the nineteenth century, and was finally sold to the Corporation in 1897 for £65,000, to become a generating station.

In 1761 foundations had been laid for the original Poolbeg Lighthouse, which was finished by 1768. It was designed by Mr. John Smith, who was also the architect of old St. Thomas's Church, Marlborough Street (1758–62) and of the sombre classic St. Catherine's in Thomas Street (1760–9), the scene of Robert Emmet's execution in 1803. From the lighthouse a line of timber piles was carried across the South Bull sand to the Pidgeon House, and then this was gradually replaced with the present stone wall. Since the

54   The roofs of Dublin, looking East from Guinness's brewery

55 Vice-regal Lodge, now Árus an Uachtaráin. Built in 1751; the wings, 1808, and the portico, 1816, were added by Francis Johnston

completion of the wall the harbour entrance has been one of the safest in the world, but the development of trade has been such that there is now too little accommodation in the port within. It is common to see several ships anchored out in the Bay, awaiting their turns at the quays, and it is clear that additional docks will have to be built in the area north of the channel to keep pace with Dublin's growing importance.

Returning from the Poolbeg light to Dublin, the road turns inland at the entrance to the Grand Canal Dock, leading to Ringsend and so either back into Pearse Street, or southwards to the not very savoury Irishtown, at the base of the curious spit or tongue of land which separates the course of the Dodder from the sea. It was this spit or *rinn* that gave Ringsend its mongrel name. In the eighteenth century, before the building of the Grand Canal and the transformation of the mouth of the Dodder, there was here a wide expanse of water extending from where the railway now runs, out to shipyards and fishermen's cabins at Ringsend and Irishtown.

West of the Grand Canal starts Sir John Rogerson's Quay on the south side of the Liffey, running on to City Quay until Butt Bridge is reached. These quays are scenes of immense activity throughout the day, similar to that of any other great port; but in the evening they take on their own special character, with the pale clear air casting its magic over the grimy pubs and warehouses and the noisy clanging of cranes and derricks giving place to the cheerful mudlarking and fighting of Dublin's irrepressible youngsters. On the nights when the Liverpool boats leave from the North Wall with their crowds of modern emigrants—lured by England's streets paved with gold—there is always a silent group on the opposite quays to watch and perhaps to follow slowly as the ship moves down the channel. For seven or eight centuries the Irish Problem was that of the immigrant; the English and other foreigners who dispossessed the natives of their birthright. But since the Potato Famine, one hundred years ago, the real problem has been that of the ever-open door leading outwards—of the Irish men and women, especially the brightest and best of Irish youth, who cannot find enough opportunities at home, or even food, and sail or steam away into the unknown. It is the shadow of this problem that lies across the faces of the watchers who follow the wake of the Liverpool boat.

If the best time to see the eastern quays is in the cool and quiet of the evening, the bright sunshine of an early summer's morning shows off to most advantage the course of the river through the city, and if the tide is high, so much the better. Of the Liffey itself the colour is the remarkable thing; totally unlike the muddy clay brown of the Thames, it possesses the translucent depths of the bogwater that supplies it and the porter into which it is transmuted. By the Four Courts, between the bridges of Father Mathew and O'Donovan Rossa, it still runs in the deep black pool, *dubh linn*, whose fame has so spread around the globe, and contrasting with the dark-eyed waters there may be a family of the swans, who share with seagulls the alms of the passers-by. Across the river bed below this pool stretches the reef of outcrop rock known as Standfast Dick, which provides a firm foundation for the Castle and the City Hall. This reef was the ancient limit of shipping, and so one of the vital factors in determining the position of the city.

The bridges are constantly changing name, and it is difficult for the stranger to follow references from one book to another. The first or Old Bridge was that built in 1210 on the site of the present Father Mathew Bridge; it fell in 1385 and on the 9th of January following the men of Dublin were granted the right to maintain a ferry for four years. Soon afterwards John More, mason, and Nicholas Mason, were ordered to arrest masons sufficient to repair the bridge "on account of the damage to the citizens by the breaking down of the bridge". This fourteenth-century bridge lasted into the nineteenth century, when in 1818 it was replaced by Whitworth Bridge, which now commemorates Father Mathew. No other bridge existed until 1670, when Bloody Bridge was built at the then western extremity of the suburbs; it was rebuilt as Barrack Bridge in 1704 and again as Victoria Bridge in 1863 —now Rory O'More Bridge. In 1683 two new bridges were made, one each side of the Old Bridge: Arran Bridge upstream, and Ormond Bridge to the east. Arran Bridge, later known as Bridewell Bridge and then as Ellis's Bridge, was rebuilt as Queen's Bridge in 1768, and is now Queen Maev Bridge— Ormond Bridge was rebuilt as Richmond Bridge in 1816, has been renamed for O'Donovan Rossa. Slightly earlier than the last two was Essex Bridge, built in line with Capel Street in 1676, rebuilt in 1755 and again as Grattan Bridge, in 1874. The graceful iron footbridge built as Wellington Bridge in

1816 was later generally known as Metal Bridge and is now Liffey Bridge (**145**). The final and greatest achievement of Dublin improvement was the building of Carlisle Bridge (**144**) in 1794, as a direct link with Sackville Street and the newly fashionable north-eastern quarter of the city. The bridge was rebuilt on its present magnificent plan, preserving the full width and level of O'Connell Street, in 1880. It was the Corporation's intention to give the name of O'Connell to the new bridge and to the whole of Sackville Street, but influential residents revolted and made an application to the courts, with the result that on the 19th of June 1885 Vice-Chancellor Chatterton granted a perpetual injunction against the Corporation to prevent the change of name. The resisters of innovation continued to call the new bridge by its old name of Carlisle Bridge for a long time, and Sackville Street is still frequently so called. The bridge preserves some of the masonry and the fine Portland-stone balustrades of its predecessor but unfortunately a good deal of the parapet is in a shaky condition, with cracked balusters tied up with battens and wire.

A year before the rebuilding of Carlisle Bridge, Butt Bridge had been opened in 1879 beside the Custom House. This has since remained the lowest of Dublin's road bridges, and is likely to remain so, for the port can hardly retreat farther towards the sea. With the exception of George Papworth's hideous King's Bridge of 1827–8, far upstream near the Park Gate, Dublin's bridges are a fine series, ranging from the satisfactory to the admirable. Queen Maev Bridge, built in 1768, is the only one left from the period of spacious architecture, but all of them are gracious structures of pleasing lines and mark with their own rhythm the curving line of the quays. Just as the eastern reaches of the river are dominated by the Custom House (**50**), so are the western by the Four Courts (**60**), Gandon's other masterpiece. Externally, it has been restored to the form of the original, largely destroyed in the fighting of 1922, as the Custom House was in the preceding year. Purists with long memories complain that the new saucer dome of the Four Courts is less satisfying than its predecessor; certainly comparison of photographs suggests that the new dome rises too high.

The restoration of the Dublin Custom House, Four Courts, and General Post Office after their partial destruction between

1916 and 1922 gave rise to much controversy on the aesthetic principle involved. It was held on the one hand that these monuments of the "British" ascendancy were architecturally unsuitable to the new Irish Dublin, and that they should be replaced with buildings of a completely Irish character (whatever that might be); while others, uninterested in the national aspect, felt that there was a strong case for sweeping away the ruins and building anew in the twentieth century. But for such a course to be justified, there would have had to be unusually strong evidence that the new structures would equal, even if not excel, those that they replaced, and it was one of the wisest decisions of the new Irish State to make sure of what they had. Johnston's Post Office is not quite on the level of the other two buildings, but all three are of first-class civic importance, and to an unusual degree *are* Dublin.

There are no other great buildings on the quays, though the Collins Barracks are an imposing pile not far from their western end, opposite to the great yard and wharves of Guinness's Brewery, and St. Paul's Catholic Church (1835–7) on Arran Quay (**31**), a Greek Ionic tetrastyle temple surmounted by an unusual cupola, adds an almost Mediterranean touch to the scene. For the rest, the quays are diversified by shops of many kinds, several hotels, a number of booksellers, and the Papal Optician's premises, a noteworthy tribute to the excellence of Dublin's optical work. Though hardly any of the riverside houses are of particular distinction, the majority are good unpretentious Georgian brickwork, and in the centre of the city many are brightly painted.

Walking along the southern quays with a map one may easily follow the extensions of building development. At the Old Bridge, just west of the Four Courts, the primaeval highway crosses the river, coming down Bridge Street within the walls of the mediaeval city, and winding its way through Church Street and up Constitution Hill towards Finglas, Glasnevin, and the north County Dublin. The Church of Church Street is of course St. Michan's (**157**), the only ancient church on the north side. It remained the only north Dublin parish until 1697, when St. Paul's and St. Mary's were formed from its western and eastern parts respectively. Church Street is a narrow and twisting thoroughfare, still with a slightly countrified manner about it, and suits well with the derivation of the old Irish road, the *bóthar*, from the wanderings

56 Kingsbridge Station, 1844. Sancton Wood, architect

57 Harcourt Street Station, 1859. G. Wilkinson, architect

58   The Phoenix Pillar in the Phoenix Park, 1747

of a driven cow (*bó*). Two blocks eastwards, a story of planned
development is told by the line of Capel Street, 40 feet wide
and almost straight, approached across Essex (now Grattan)
Bridge by Parliament Street, laid out in 1757 (**59**). Capel
Street itself had been started about 1675, and was practically
complete by 1710. The next extension was an even bigger
stride, to Sackville Street, set out in 1750, and linked to the
south bank by Gandon's Carlisle Bridge in 1794. There is as it
were a geometrical progression in the scale of ideas as the
successive steps are taken: Church Street to Capel Street is as
Capel Street to O'Connell Street. The Wide Streets Commissioners and their architect James Gandon had a grandeur
and breadth of view in their ideas which is not likely to be
excelled.

Continuing along the river, the east to west axis of the
city, we reach Kingsbridge Station (**56**) and the Phoenix
Park (**58**). By the good fortune of history, the great western
demesne of the Knights Hospitallers of mediaeval Kilmainham
has itself been preserved from building development and has
thus set a limit to Dublin's expansion in this direction. At
the same time the land itself provides the most splendid park
in Europe in immediate adjacency to a capital. The Park
Gate is little over one and a half miles from the Loop Line
Railway Bridge—that is roughly the same distance that the
Admiralty Arch in London is from the railway bridge into
Cannon Street Station. The Phoenix Park contains 1,752
acres, an area exactly equal to the combined total of Hyde
Park, Kensington Gardens, the Green Park, St. James's
Park, Regents Park, Primrose Hill, Parliament Hill, and
Hampstead Heath. In addition there is a certain area to the
south of the Liffey which belonged to the Hospitallers'
demesne and which is permanently protected from development, including the grounds of the former Royal Hospital (**62**),
now the headquarters of the Civic Guard.

Within the Park are several important enclosures: the
People's Garden, with an exquisite lake and bedding plants
in borders on the lines of St. James's Park—and the Zoological Gardens, with an excellent small collection of animals
and a Refreshment Room giving the best value for money
(and good value that is) in Dublin; the Vice-regal Lodge, now
the President's House or Árus an Uachtaráin (**55**); the Chief
Secretary's Lodge, now the United States Legation; the Under

Secretary's Lodge (Ashtown Castle), now the Apostolic Nunciature; Mountjoy Barrack (first the private residence of Luke Gardiner, grandfather of the first Lord Mountjoy), now the Ordnance Survey Office; the Royal Hibernian Military School, now the Coláiste Móibí; the Military Infirmary by the People's Garden, and the Civic Guard Depot and Barrack next to the Zoo. The buildings belong to the historical architecture of Dublin, but it is here desirable to give a short summary of the history of the Park itself. There was an early confusion between the name *Fionn Uisge*, clear water, applied to a spring of mineral water near the north end of the present Zoological Gardens, and the Phoenix House, which was on the south side of the Park at the site of the Magazine Fort. This house became a vice-regal residence under James I, but it was only in 1671 that the whole extent of the Park was purchased for Charles II by the Duke of Ormonde, and surrounded with a wall to preserve the deer. It was at first, like Richmond Park, Crown property with no right of public access, but in 1747 the famous Earl of Chesterfield, as Viceroy, threw it open, and the rights of the public have been constantly maintained for the last two centuries.

The magnificent main avenue runs through the Park for nearly three miles, and during the present conditions of fuel shortage is flanked each winter by enormous mounds of brown peat, or as it is known in Ireland, "turf". The singular illogicality of usage is well shown by the avoidance in Hiberno-English of the synonym "peat", in spite of the fact that "turf" is used far more commonly than in England to signify horse-racing. In fact, there is hardly a street in greater Dublin without one or more neat offices with obscured lower glazing, which might be thought estate agencies or the cool parlours of solicitors, did they not bear the discreet title of Turf Accountant, the Irish equivalent of bookmaker. The peat merchant is a Turf Factor—and while on the subject of the Anglo-Irish language, domestic crockery is delf, and a back yard is said to be "in rere" of the house to which it belongs. Bacon is known as Rashers, green spring onions are Scallions, a pram is a Car, and potatoes are sold by the stone.

No visitor to Dublin should miss the Zoo; although small compared with the London Zoo in Regents Park, Dublin excels in what one would imagine the particularly English capacity of breeding lions. The Dublin Zoo is practically the

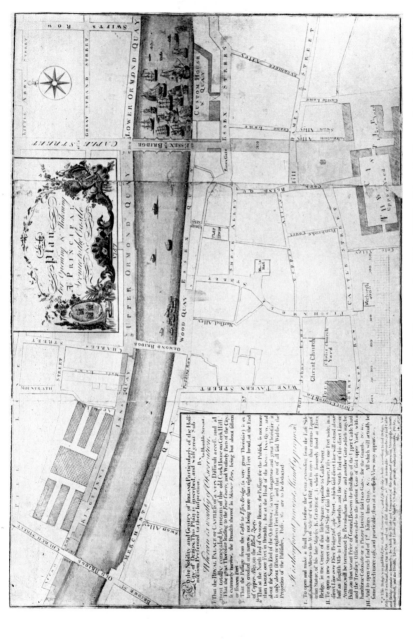

59 The plan for Parliament Street, the first work of the Wide Streets Commission, 1757

60   The Four Courts, 1786–96.   James Gandon, architect

only place in the world where lions will breed in captivity, and not only do so, but make a normal habit of it. The result in revenue and exchange value to the Dublin Zoological Society is naturally very great. Between 1857 and 1946, 131 litters of lions were born in the Gardens, making a total of 410 cubs. No one knows the secret, but lions happen to like Dublin; and certainly they are well treated, for they take turns in occupying an outdoor arena supplied with cave-like dens, and separated from the public by a deep ditch without bars. Mr. T. H. Mason informs me that some lions are so accustomed to the protection of bars that they will not emerge from the dens until they have been acclimatized by the provision of temporary sections of railings, which are removed from the front of the arena, piecemeal.

The other interesting visit in the Park is to the Ordnance Survey Office. Here are kept the main stocks of all the Eire Ordnance Maps, many of which can only be obtained to special order in the city. But quite apart from the specialist who needs large-scale or historical maps, the Office is of great interest in that it still preserves and prints from original engraved copper-plates many maps now superseded. For example, there are key-maps of the counties showing the boundaries of civil parishes, most important for historical purposes, but now obsolete for local government. The office, given a few days' warning, will print off copies of the counties required from the old plates; also obtainable are copies of the Barony Maps of Sir William Petty's famous Down Survey, photographed in 1908 from the surviving set preserved in the Bibliothèque Nationale of Paris. The Down Survey of 1655 was the first complete topographical survey of any country, and shows even the boundaries of parishes and townlands; incidentally, its name has nothing to do with the County Down, but is derived from the features of the country having been plotted *down* upon the map. The French set of the maps was captured by a privateer and in spite of repeated diplomatic protests at several periods, was never restored to Britain. Perhaps fortunately, for the original Irish maps have all been destroyed, by fires in the Custom House in 1711 and at the Record Office in the Four Courts in 1922, though a number of certified copies in the Quit-Rent Office, Dublin, have been preserved.

Just beyond and below the Phoenix Park, beside the

Liffey, lies the little village of Chapelizod (**61**), the scene of J. Sheridan Le Fanu's great story, *The House by the Churchyard*, a wonderful study, not only of nervous suspense, but of the old-time society of Dublin and its neighbourhood. Le Fanu's name, that of an old Huguenot family of Dublin, is pronounced Leffanew, with the accent on the first syllable. Chapelizod is still a charming little village around the old church tower, to which in the period of ecclesiastical rehabilitation around 1830 was attached a "spike-Gothic" church. Notwithstanding the peculiarities of this style, the result at Chapelizod is inoffensive, and certainly more praiseworthy than that of the over-large Roman Catholic Church a little on the Dublin side of the village. Returning to Dublin on the southern side of the river by the St. Lawrence Road and Inchicore Road, the grim portals of Kilmainham Gaol are passed, and soon afterwards the fancy Gothic Gate of the Royal Hospital is reached. This gate was designed by Francis Johnston, and built in 1812 at the eastern end of Victoria Quay. But after the opening of the railway from Kingsbridge in 1846, the bottleneck produced by the gate was quite throttling to traffic, and the structure was removed stone by stone to its present position. To view the Royal Hospital (**62**) a permit from the Civic Guard has to be obtained, and in order to see the interior of Hall and Chapel, which are the specially important parts both historically and architecturally, a separate permit from the National Museum. The buildings, erected between 1680 and 1686 at a cost of nearly £24,000, were for long erroneously attributed to Wren, but were really designed by Sir William Robinson, the Surveyor-General for Ireland.

The original purpose of the Hospital was the support of Army pensioners, on the same lines as Chelsea Hospital, and the pensioners continued in occupation until the setting up of the Free State in 1922, and in the case of those too feeble to be moved, for some years afterwards. The buildings became the Headquarters of the Gárda Síochána (Civic Guards), and are thus in a sense the Scotland Yard of Ireland; the Hall with its fine portraits is disused, except as an overflow store for the National Museum; and so is the Chapel, which contained some important mediaeval stained glass, now removed to safety on account of the war emergency. One of the few stray bombs which actually fell in the Dublin area came close to the

61 The Liffey at Longmeadow near Chapelizod

62   The Royal Hospital, Kilmainham, 1680-6. Sir William
Robinson, architect
From the aquatint by James Malton

63   The great courtyard of Dublin Castle
From the aquatint by James Malton

Hospital. Still visible are the plaster ceiling, and the wood-carvings, which like so many more are attributed to Grinling Gibbons, but have been shown by Mr. C. P. Curran to be the work of James Tabary, a French sculptor settled in Dublin, who was admitted to the freedom by special Act in 1685.

Close to the Royal Hospital Gateway is the old burying ground of Bully's Acre, in which still stands the shaft of the high cross of Kilmainham. This was the first of Dublin's cemeteries, and was so popular that its closure was prevented by widespread rioting in the eighteenth century; a later epidemic of cholera led to such overcrowding that it was closed by universal consent. Adjoining Bully's Acre on the north is a much smaller burying ground, allotted to the pensioners, and containing several graves of British troops who were killed in the 1916 rising. In contrast to the generally neglected and overgrown state of Irish graveyards, the neatness of this little plot is pleasant, and reflects great credit on the scrupulous care of the Board of Works for the graves of its official predecessors and, by the same token, ex-enemies. In Ireland, old rancour dies very hard indeed and conventional respect is termed hypocrisy; but there are exceptions.

The River Liffey and its quays now form the great thoroughfare through the length of Dublin, but the older route lay along the ridge of the hill parallel to the river's south bank. This is the eastern end of a line of low hills stretching right across the great plain of Ireland, and it was this line which formed the frontier between the two halves of Ireland at Dublin's first emergence into history, about A.D. 150. Mogh, King of Munster, defeated his overlord Conn the Hundred-Fighter, or "of the Hundred Battles", and enforced a treaty by which Conn was left with only that part of Ireland to the north of this line, which was continued eastwards through the High Street of Dublin. Although Mogh later repudiated the treaty because it left Conn in possession of Dublin's already valuable harbour, the division of Ireland into Conn's half and Mogh's half was long remembered, and the very name Munster contains a corruption of the name of its early ruler Mogh.

Following this ancient boundary we first traverse Kilmainham Lane, descend to cross the little River Cammock at Bow Bridge, and climb again to James's Street, which is reached at the top of Steevens Lane. Here stands St. Patrick's

Hospital, the home for lunatics founded under the terms of Swift's famous bequest, and at the bottom of the lane is Madame Grissel Steevens' Hospital (24), the first of Dublin's modern infirmaries, begun in 1720 and opened in 1733. "Madame" Steevens (she was in fact a spinster) provides one of the stock Dublin stories; her mother is said to have been pestered by a beggarwoman with a tribe of children, characterized by Mrs. Steevens as being like an old sow with her litter. The beggar's curse is supposed to have resulted in Mrs. Steevens' next child, a daughter Grissel, being born with a pig's snout. Grissel Steevens disproved the story by sitting frequently at her open window, but it is still quoted from time to time as an instance of a monstrous birth. The hospital carries on its work in the original building, which forms a delightful cloistered quadrangle. Smartly uniformed nurses flit to and fro, but the calm repose within the doors seems to offer better hope of health and rest than the echoing vaults and bustle of many more modern institutions.

James's Street leads past the entrance of Guinness's and becomes Thomas Street, which runs by the site of St. Thomas's Abbey (64). The Abbey Liberty after the dissolution became that of the Earl of Meath, and the Meath Liberty is implied when "The Liberty" is mentioned in records. Owing to the freedom from the city regulations, the Liberty became a centre of free craftsmen who were not tied to the restrictive companies; the great industry, largely manned by French Huguenots, was that of the weavers, and it was their apprentices who were the notorious "Liberty Boys". Until recent years this quarter was the least altered in the whole of Dublin: Meath Street, Ardee Street, Weaver Square, The Coombe, all were filled with old houses of the late seventeenth and early eighteenth centuries. Now all have been swept away in the interest of civic hygiene. There are still, among squalid nineteenth-, and uninteresting twentieth-century houses, a few relics of the past. In Mill Street, at the bottom of Mill Lane is a fine old house of purple brick, wrecked by the addition of a hideous top storey. Except to the enthusiast of slum clearance, the Liberty cannot now be said to present much of interest to match its former importance and beauty.

Thomas Street is one of Dublin's magnificently wide highways, and is rather a type of the great Irish provincial towns of one main street, than a mere section of the capital. It has

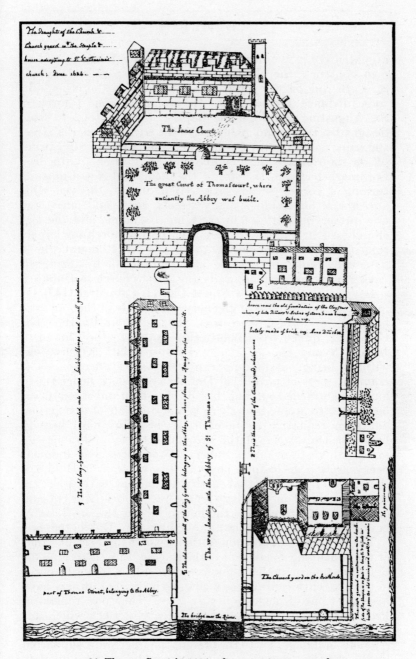

The draught of the Church &
Church yard w.th the Steeple &
house adioyning to S.t Kathrenis
church; Anno 1634.

The Inner Courte

The great Court of Thomascourt, where
anciantly the Abbey waf built.

heere was the old foundation of the Cloyfters
whereof late Pillars & Arches of stone have beene
taken up.

lately made of brick ou.r Anno Dm. 1634

9. The old long garden, now conuerted into diuers fraitbuildings and small gardens.

6. The old meane wall of the long Garden belonging to the Abbey, on whose place the stony Houses are built.

The way leading onto the Abbey of S.t Thomas

2 Thus the new wall of the Church yard, which was

He presentmd.

The Church yard on the Northside.

part of Thomas Street, belonging to the Abbey.

The bridge over the Riuer.

64 Thomas Court in 1634, after a contemporary plan

an extensive assortment of shops, a Public Library, and its own churches: the old Church of Ireland parish church of St. Catherine on the south side (**90**), and on the other side, some distance farther east, the great Catholic Church of SS. Augustine and John the Baptist, built in 1862–72 from designs by Pugin and Ashlin. At the eastern end the street suddenly narrows into Cornmarket, and Francis Street runs off on the right to the Coombe and St. Patrick's Cathedral. Cornmarket crosses the site of the mediaeval New Gate and turning a corner becomes the High Street—the venerable ancestor of all Dublin's many streets, roads and lanes, and now preserving little of interest but its name, and the two churches of St. Audoen: the mediaeval parish church now largely ruined (**156**), and immediately to the east, its Roman Catholic namesake built in 1841–6, and considered by Professor Abercrombie as architecturally the finest church in Dublin.

Beyond High Street is Christ Church Cathedral (**143**) set in its little public park of greenery, on the site of the monastic buildings and their successors, the old Four Courts. The Cathedral, linked by a neo-Gothic bridge to the Church of Ireland Synod House, was over-restored last century, but without being outstanding can still inspire affection. The cramped ways of mediaeval Dublin which once hedged it in have been widened out, but the tide of fashion and of commerce has retreated so far that there is a strange air of dereliction, not even realizable in London in the areas most heavily bombed. Only some of the provincial towns of France can match this strange atmosphere of shiftless and indolent decay around an historic church. The contrast in Dublin is the more striking in that both the ancient cathedrals are themselves kept in excellent repair and spotlessly swept and garnished condition, as is the delightful old Marsh's Library beside St. Patrick's, the first public library in Dublin (**65, 66**).

The ecclesiastical position of the two cathedrals is, like that of the remaining mediaeval cathedrals of Eire, a sore point. Catholics point out that they were seized by a minority party in the sixteenth century, and that their original owners have been kept out of possession ever since. They now remain in Protestant hands in virtue of the Treaty of 1922, which forbade any change in the denominational ownership of existing religious buildings. Up to the present the Irish State, supported by the good-natured majority of the population, has honoured

66 Interior

65 Exterior

MARSH'S LIBRARY, BUILT 1703, FOUNDED AS A LIBRARY 1707. Sir William Robinson, architect

67   The great Gate of Dublin Castle, with the figure of Justice

this clause, but the continued thinning of the Protestant ranks has caused considerable qualms, though not necessarily of conscience. So long as the Church of Ireland continues to be, as it is now, a body of intellectual and professional strength in Dublin, it is likely to retain its ancient churches, regardless of the means by which it obtained them. It is even possible that the new silent invasion of Englishmen may cancel out the diminution in the Protestant ranks, and indefinitely prolong the present *status quo*.

Lord Edward Street leads on to the Castle Gates (**67**), the City Hall (**89**), and Dame Street, the concluding section of this great west-to-east way. The Castle, for over seven centuries the mainspring of Dublin life, is so no more. Though used for a number of ceremonial purposes such as the reception of foreign ministers, when its yards rattle and clash with the Ruritanian Blue Hussar guard of honour, the Castle is now mainly a collection of government offices of relatively little importance. The former Chapel Royal is now the Catholic Church of the Most Holy Trinity: it was built to the design of Francis Johnston (1807–14) in a peculiar style of gingerbread Gothic which has little to recommend it except the one characteristic—novelty—which it has inevitably lost by lapse of time. But even as a novelty the Chapel Royal could hardly have ranked with Strawberry Hill, Fonthill Abbey, or the Brighton Pavilion.

The one really interesting thing at the Castle, apart from the departed glory of the State Apartments, preserved like a wedding cake beneath a glass bell, is the Genealogical Office (**70**). As Mr. Harold Leask points out in the official guidebook, the core of the building, on which rests the graceful cupola (mid-eighteenth century), is the western drum-tower of the mediaeval Castle Gatehouse. The unique heraldic and genealogical museum owes almost everything to the efforts of the late Sir Nevile Wilkinson during his long term of office as Ulster King of Arms; it contains a fine representative collection of seals, banners, illuminated grants of arms, pedigrees, heraldic china and glass, and many association pieces. There is also a most valuable map, still in course of amplification, showing the territories occupied in Ireland by the various families of natives and invaders. As the Norman families are shown in a distinct colour, the extent of their penetration of the country can be seen immediately.

Just before the Castle gate stands the City Hall, once the Royal Exchange, designed by Thomas Cooley and built at a cost of £40,000 between 1769 and 1779 (**89**). Cooley came from London after winning an open competition for the Dublin Exchange, and regarded as a civic ornament it is a rich and stately termination to the vista of Parliament Street. It suffers as a building from the defect of so many monuments of classic show, that its accommodation is awkward and unsuitable, most of its space being given over to the admirable domed hall which cannot now be made to serve any purpose other than that of a sculpture gallery and waiting room. John Hogan's statue of O'Connell, and the portrait figure of Dr. Charles Lucas with which Edward Smyth made his reputation, are well worth seeing (**74, 75**). Smyth is more famous for his work on the sculptures of the Custom House (**17**), where he was employed by Gandon at the suggestion of Henry Darley, the general contractor.

On the other side of Cork Hill are the Municipal Buildings (**33**), formerly Newcomen's Bank, a delicate and rather Adamesque design by Thomas Ivory, the architect of the Blue-Coat School (**8**) on the other side of the Liffey. Newcomen's Bank was designed in 1781, when the Blue-Coat School was nearing completion; the bank building has an exquisite quality of precision about its workmanship, and provides the needed foil to Cooley's heavier, rather grandiose Exchange. Ivory was the only member of the great quadrumvirate of Irish Georgian architecture who could honestly be called Irish. Gandon and Cooley both came from England; Francis Johnston was of Scottish extraction; but Ivory began his career as a carpenter in Cork, and his work is not merely satisfying to the eye, but has the sound structural sense of the competent skilled craftsman behind it. Undoubtedly one of the chief reasons for the success of Dublin's eighteenth-century street architecture is that it was largely designed, not by amateurs at drawing boards, but by masons, bricklayers and carpenters with a solid background of technical knowledge. Thus Dublin was able to carry onwards the impression of genuineness often absent from London work of the same period.

There are still a few fine old fronts among the hugger-mugger of modern shops and offices that make up Dame Street, which, leading from the Castle to College Green (**27**),

48

68   Dublin Castle: the Throne Room, remodelled by Francis Johnston

69   Trinity College: the Drawing Room of the Provost's Lodge, 1760
John Smith, architect, after designs by the Earl of Burlington

70   Dublin Castle: the garrison in the 1840's, before the Office of Arms,
     now the Genealogical Office. Thomas Ivory, architect
From a photograph by W. H. Fox-Talbot

was in the days of the later Viceroys one of the most important streets in the city. It still has a solid backbone of banks and insurance offices, many of them housed in specimens of the epidemic of supposedly Ruskinian "Gothic" which beset Dublin after the success of Benjamin Woodward's remarkable Engineering School (**119, 120**) at Trinity College (1853–5) and his Kildare Street Clubhouse (1859–61). Woodward's Lombardo-Venetian work is pardonable, and even in parts impressive, but the tail-end of the Revival poured out on Dublin its most horrifyingly unsuitable types, so that one shudders and passes by, willing to forget!

Dame Street is closed by the main front of Trinity College (**91**), built in 1752–60 from the designs of Henry Keene and John Sanderson, two more of London's loans to Dublin, who could build far better in the inspiration of Irish air than they could in their native England. The front of T.C.D. is perhaps too stiff and frigid—one of the most English of Irish buildings—but it is on a grand scale practically unknown to London, and suggesting the magnificence of Vienna or Munich. Setting aside the front of Christ Church, Oxford, of an utterly different period and style, this is the one truly monumental piece of collegiate architecture in the British Isles, and it has besides the advantage of fronting on an ample space, with another fine building on the flank, the old Parliament House (**71, 72**). As we see it now, the Parliament House transformed into the Bank of Ireland is a queer jigsaw of several periods. The original design has been further altered by the results of the fire of 1792, which destroyed the important dome over the House of Commons. What we have consists of the original House of Lords and main entrance front, with the central House of Commons (**77**) as transformed by Vincent Waldré and again altered for Bank purposes; the East Portico to the House of Lords, designed by Gandon and begun in 1785, with its curving screen wall, to which engaged columns were attached by Francis Johnston in 1803; and the West Portico in Foster Place, first designed by Gandon, but actually carried out by Robert Park from plans said to have been partly "devised" by Samuel Hayes, then M.P. for Maryborough, in 1797; and the Cash Office inserted by Johnston behind the main entrance, between 1803 and 1808. The original building was begun in 1729 under Edward Lovett Pearce, who was knighted in 1732 and died in the following year; and completed by his successor in the Surveyor-Generalship, Arthur Dobbs, in 1739. The first design was probably made by Thomas Burgh, Pearce's predecessor as Surveyor-General, and designer of the Library at Trinity College, who died soon after the work began, but there seems to be no truth in the often repeated statement that the real architect was the German settler, Richard Cassels, whose plans are said to have been appropriated or plagiarized by Pearce. Mr. Thomas Sadleir, who has studied the problem in great detail, has shown how improbable this story is, and gives the credit to Pearce, who had certainly visited Italy and produced drawings with his own hand.

The interior can be viewed without appointment, and though there is little else of interest, it is worth while to do so in order to see the magnificent tapestries still hanging in the former House of Lords. They were completed and hung in 1735 by John van Beaver and his assistants, working for Robert Baillie of Dublin, and cost £436 6s. 3d. One piece depicts the Battle of the Boyne, and the other the Siege of Derry, and both are still in excellent condition and fresh colour. Various other mementoes of the "Old House" are preserved, as well as some early cheques, and mint specimens of the Irish coinage. The Bank, as principal agent of the sterling connexion, remains a stronghold of "West British" views, and as such a thorn in the flesh to earnest republicans. And while I am on the subject, I must say a few words on the strange misuse of the term British in Ireland, and the absolutely uncalled-for paroxysms which it can evoke. Even if the English do take a lot for granted in their attitude to what have been picturesquely termed the "lesser breeds without the law", nobody outside of Ireland would ever dream that *British* implied anything more than a geographical conception: the inhabitants of the British Isles and what is theirs. Its wide adoption in place of *English* has been directly due to the pardonable objection of the Scots and Welsh to being included as "Englishmen" in the mouths of foreigners. But the Irish, even those who are not in other respects extremists, refuse to be connected even geographically with England, and for them Ireland must be for ever sundered from the rest of that island group of which upon the map it forms so obvious a part. Still more, the phrase "West British" has been employed as a term of violent abuse, directed at all those who believed in the slightest degree of co-operation with England, rather than

72   Bank Messengers

THE BANK OF IRELAND, FORMERLY THE PARLIAMENT HOUSE

71   Foster Place

75 Dr. Charles Lucas
Edward Smyth, sculptor

74 Daniel O'Connell
John Hogan, sculptor

STATUARY IN THE CITY HALL

73 Henry Grattan
Sir Francis Chantrey, sculptor

one-hundred per cent isolation. "The British" in many an Irish mouth has implications only equalled by those of *les boches* in France; it is one of the few sad instances where the Irish sense of humour is lost.

At Trinity College we come to the end of the road: in the daytime we may enter the gates, between the statues of Burke and Goldsmith, both by John Henry Foley, and the latter especially one of his finest works (7). Facing them in College Green is his statue of Grattan, with eloquent hand upraised. Through the cobbled Parliament Square, Library Square is reached, with the great Library block on the right (10), and beyond it the College Park, through which one may wander, past the playing field, to a gate leading into Lincoln Place, close to Westland Row, with its Catholic Church (32) and important railway station. Almost adjacent to Lincoln Place is the north-west corner of Merrion Square, linked directly to the foot of Grafton Street and College Green by Nassau Street—long ago known as Patrick's Well Lane, from a famous holy well, now lost. At the Grafton Street end of Nassau Street, opposite to the high wall round the Provost's Garden, is Jammet's, the fashionable French restaurant, and half-way along it is the Kildare Street Club on the corner of the street of like name. We have now seen most of the Dublin that lies along the river axis, and it is time to change direction and move from north to south.

As I remarked earlier, there are three main cross routes of traffic, each representing a stage in historic development: O'Connell Street, Capel Street, and Church Street. Taking the first and most important, we find at its northern extremity Parnell (Rutland) Square, containing that social landmark the Rotunda Hospital (22, 130), and on its far side the Municipal Art Gallery housed in Charlemont House (12) and the up-to-date galleries built out behind it. Parnell Square, once a fashionable quarter, and centred on the gaiety and shows of the Rotunda Gardens, is now drab enough, but the gardens contain trees and grass, in spite of the encroachments of the hospital extensions and nurses' quarters. Running off to the north-east is Great Denmark Street with Belvedere House, now a Jesuit College, and beyond that again, and farther north, Temple Street leading into Hardwicke Place with St. George's Church (40), by some considered Francis Johnston's greatest contribution to Dublin.

South of Parnell Square stretches the splendid breadth of O'Connell Street, with its focus at the Nelson Pillar and the General Post Office as its most notable building, again the work of Johnston (**45**). Not much else is left from the former glory of Sackville Street (**44**), for the combined fury of the risings and civil wars of 1916, 1921 and 1922 left little but wreckage. The new buildings of the street, without being positively objectionable, have little distinction. But in Cathal Brugha Street stands a pleasant little neo-Byzantine church designed by Mr. F. G. Hicks, taking the place of burnt-out St. Thomas's. Close to O'Connell Street and near the middle of its east side stands the Catholic Pro-Cathedral (1816–25) designed by John Sweetman of Raheny, a simple and unpretentious Greek Doric building with a central dome (**79, 80**). Near the bottom of the street Abbey Street crosses, and at the beginning of the second block from O'Connell Street is the Abbey Theatre (**28**), which possibly symbolizes more than any other single building the real values behind the new Ireland. Only a few doors away there stood until 1916 the Royal Hibernian Academy, one of the most tragic of the cultural losses of the Rebellion.

Across the bridge, D'Olier Street swings left and connects with Pearse (Great Brunswick) Street and Townshend Street (once Lazar's Hill) at the Crampton Monument, at the site where the Long Stone of the Ostmen once stood. Forking right from D'Olier Street, Westmoreland Street leads directly to the Bank of Ireland and Trinity College, while College Street closes the triangle to the Crampton Monument. At the opening of College Street stands a statue of Thomas Moore, notebook in hand. Past the front of the College, the line is continued by Grafton Street, the one fashionable shopping street of Dublin, but narrow and winding. Steadily rising, it opens into the north-west corner of St. Stephen's Green (**113**), said to be the largest city square in Europe, and certainly the finest. The west side has been tinged with commercialism by the spread of shops, but the erstwhile mansions of the aristocracy are now become clubs, offices, or University hostels.

Within the Green itself are a lake, waterfalls, fountains, gardens, glass-plots, almost a forest of trees, and a few statues. The most famous, and artistically the most important of the statues was that of George II on horseback, by John Van Nost, but it has been destroyed by political hooligans; there are still busts of James Clarence Mangan the poet (**18**), a dismally bad one of Countess Markievicz, political leader and rebel of 1916, and Tom Kettle, who strangely enough was killed fighting as a British soldier in the Great War of 1914–18. On the west side of the Green is the Royal College of Surgeons (1825–27) (**23**), and a large part of the south side is given up to university premises, including the important Georgian houses, Nos. 85 and 86, and Cardinal Newman's Byzantine University Church (1854–6) (**161**). The interior of this church, while comically unsuitable to Dublin, and typifying Newman's aloof and humourless character, has points of real beauty, and succeeds in capturing with extraordinary fidelity the atmosphere of its prototypes. The architect, who leaned upon Newman to an unusual degree, was John Hungerford Pollen.

Beyond St. Stephen's Green the line of thoroughfare moves on in a majestic sweeping curve through Harcourt Street to the South Circular Road and the terminus of the old Dublin, Wicklow and Wexford Railway. Harcourt Street was laid out between 1775 and 1791, at the highest peak of Irish Georgian culture, and it remains most impressive, with its serried ranks of rich purple-brick houses. The station is practically the last of the Classic buildings of the old tradition, built in 1859, and comprising a Roman Doric piazza of most Mediterranean appearance broken in the centre by a grand semicircular arch surmounted by a pediment and flanked and abutted by inverted consoles. Squalid the station has certainly become, but it is not "ornamental" in the sense of Yeats's sneer: as classic railway stations go it is a pronounced success, and all the better for its small scale and avoidance of pretentiousness and pompous display (**57**).

A few yards of the Circular Road brings us to the Rathmines Road, the older southern outlet of the east side of the city. This crosses the Grand Canal at Portobello Bridge, beside which is Portobello Harbour on the Canal, and standing by the harbour the former Grand Canal Hotel, a grandiose building of three stories which, with others at the important points served by the Canal, formed part of the great system of communication which linked Ireland for a generation and more before the coming of the railway (**82**). There will be more to say of this system in relation to the growth of the city, but for the present the Canal makes a suitable ending to our cross-Dublin route.

By turning at Portobello Bridge, and re-entering Dublin through Camden Street, we are following the second of the main routes. From narrow Camden Row on the left a glimpse can be had of the ruins of St. Kevin's Church, in the midst of one of the overgrown and locked graveyards that are a disgrace to Ireland. Farther on, Whitefriars Street forks left, and here stands the Church and Priory of the Calced Carmelites, on the same site as its mediaeval forerunner. This is the only instance in Dublin of a religious order having recovered its original position, and most appropriately it is here that the late mediaeval oak statue of Our Lady of Dublin is preserved (**84**). According to tradition, this belonged to St. Mary's Cistercian Abbey north of the Liffey, and was preserved after partial burning by hollowing out the back and using it face down as a hog-trough. Miss Catriona MacLeod compares the statue to those of the opening years of the sixteenth century in Henry VII's Chapel, and suggests that it belongs to the last few years before the dissolution. As it now stands, above the Lady altar in the North Chapel of the Carmelite Church, in the light of hundreds of votive candles, this statue is one of the unforgettable sights of Dublin.

At the foot of Whitefriars Street, the right fork is Aungier Street, and here at No. 12 was the birthplace of Thomas Moore in 1779. A little farther on and the street, with a double curve, becomes South Great Georges Street, an important shopping centre, with the South City Market on the right. A right turn into Lower Stephen Street, and second left, brings us to William Street, where on the right hand is Powerscourt House (**34**), now the premises of Messrs. Ferrier and Pollock. It is one of the finest and least spoiled of the houses of the grand manner, built in 1771–4 from a design by Robert Mack, another of Dublin's obscure but supremely competent master builders. William Street leads on to St. Andrew's parish church, a painstaking but not unpleasing modern Gothic building (1860–73), the drawings for which, by "Lanyon, Lynn & Lanyon", are in the National Library. The church stands on the site of the Nunnery of St. Mary de Hogge, so called from the mound or "hogge" that formed the great meeting place or Thengmote of the Norse citizens of Dublin. It rose 40 feet above the general level of the ground

76   The Volunteers of the City and County of Dublin on College Green, 4 November 1779

From the water-colour by Francis Wheatley

77 The Irish House of Commons in 1790, with John Philpot Curran speaking. Built 1729-39: Sir Edward Lovett Pearce, architect
From the painting by Henry Barraud and John Hayter

and was 224 feet in circumference. Until the seventeenth century it stood in an open common, but the city authorities gradually enclosed and leased it off, plot by plot, until the mount itself was levelled in 1682. Fortunately an exact plan of the plot in which it stood had been made, and shows that it was immediately north-east of the present St. Andrew's Church, in the corner of Church Lane and Suffolk Street (78).

The end of Dame Street and the lower part of Cork Hill intervene between the head of South Great Georges Street and its northward continuation, Parliament Street. This results from the lie of the land and the position of the Castle, which is a terminus to the Capel Street –Parliament Street line. The chief interest of Capel Street is its period flavour— it has still an old-world atmosphere, in which plain decent human beings go about their leisurely business, shopping and gossiping and passing the time of day. Though the street has seen better

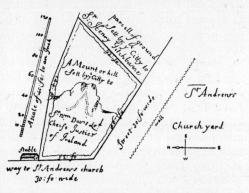

78 Plan of the Thengmote (Thing Mount) before levelling, c. 1680

days, and lies in the middle of a decaying area, it is still neat enough not to be depressing, as are so many of the streets of the north city. As Thomas Street is to west Dublin, and Great Georges Street to the south, so Capel Street is the main shopping centre of its own quarter: unlike Henry Street, Moore Street and Talbot Street, all close to the General Post Office, which are surging centres of attraction for bargain shoppers from the whole area of the city and suburbs. The upper end of Capel Street leads to Dorset Street, with Sheridan's birthplace, and to the famous streets of the higher ground: Henrietta Street, Dominick Street, St. Mary's Place with the extraordinary Black Church (1829–30) by John Semple (159), and at the very top Johnston's Eccles Street (40) and the Mater Misericordiae Hospital on the site of the intended Royal Circus. All of this region is now in sombre desolation, relieved by the shining paint and excellent repair of a few of the finest houses, now become charitable and religious institutions.

A few yards off Capel Street is the finest and least spoilt relic of mediaeval Dublin: the vaulted Chapter House of St. Mary's Abbey (**149**). For many years it was divided into two storehouses by an inserted floor, but it has recently been cleared and properly consolidated by the Office of Public Works, and is a National Monument. It can be viewed on application to the caretaker who lives a few yards away in Mary's Abbey. The chamber is 45 feet long and 24 feet in span, and has a grand and simple vault with moulded cross- and groin-ribs. According to Mr. Harold Leask the rib-mouldings are closely paralleled by those of the Chapter House of Buildwas Abbey, Shropshire, the mother house of St. Mary's Abbey, and indicate a date about A.D. 1180. Apart from its great beauty, the room has historical interest as the supposed scene of the defiance of "Silken Thomas" in 1534. Lord Thomas Fitzgerald, so called from his love of fine cloth-ing, was acting as Lord Deputy during the absence of his father, and presided at a meeting of the Council, when he heard a false rumour that his father had been executed by Henry VIII. He flung down the Sword of State upon the Council board and renounced his allegiance, as a preliminary to a three-years' rebellion which led to his own death and the execution of five of his uncles.

From the upper part of Dorset Street it is easy to reach the North Circular Road through Eccles Street or Berkeley Road, and so to take the Phibsborough Road to the Glasnevin Botanic Gardens. The gardens are not on the grand scale of Kew, but cover 50 acres of undulating ground sloping down to the little River Tolka. They were started by the Royal Dublin Society in 1795 "to increase and foster a taste for practical and scientific botany", and excellently well they have served their purpose for a century and a half, besides con-tributing greatly to the pleasure and enjoyment of the general public. The Tolka in its sudden little valley is to north Dublin what the Dodder is to the south side, though it lies much closer in to the centre. Both rivers interrupt the otherwise unending spread of suburban houses, which in the past fifty years have ruined so much of Dublin's countryside. For-tunately, the suburbs are neither so dense nor so industrialized

80 Interior

79 Exterior

ST. MARY'S CATHOLIC PRO-CATHEDRAL, 1816–25. John Sweetman, architect

81   Harcourt Lock on the Grand Canal

From an aquatint by J. J. Barralet

82   The Grand Canal Hotel, Portobello, *c.* 1807

as those of London, and everywhere there are glimpses of
green fields and of the distant hills.

Our final trip across Dublin takes us down the spacious
slope of the Phibsborough Road, crossed at the Broadstone
Station by an impressive viaduct (39). This used to be the
Foster Aqueduct, carrying a branch of the Royal Canal to its
high-level harbour, afterwards superseded by the Midland
Great Western Railway goods station. The terminus is no
longer in use, and is converted to a bus garage, but the main
building of 1850, by John Skipton Mulvany, still stands (21).
It should indeed be carefully preserved, for it is the most
original of the Dublin railway stations, a pleasing and simple
granite block of modified Greek Doric type, with a grand
Egyptianesque pylon for central feature and entry. By the
yard gates the Midland Great Western Railway Company
(dead these five-and-twenty years) still gives notice to the
drivers of Hackney Carriages that they are not to enter until
fifteen minutes before the arrival of the train.

Mulvany was the son of Thomas James Mulvany, the
admiring biographer of Gandon, and the Broadstone shows
how Gandon's lessons of scale and composition had been well
learnt. A realization of some of the monstrosities being
perpetrated elsewhere in 1850 should make us value the enduring strength of the Anglo-Irish tradition.

The name of the Broadstone doubtless perpetuates another
of the boundary or assembly points of the Norsemen, but the
exact site of the stone has been lost; the part of the road
immediately north of the Foster Aqueduct was known as
Broad Stone before the coming of the railway. From the
present roadway above the arch there is a splendid view over
the city, and in particular of the King's Inns set just below
in their green open space (39). The original design for the
King's Inns was made by Gandon, and some work was done
between 1795 and 1798; but it seems that the main building
was not begun until 1802, and was carried on by Gandon's
pupil H. A. Baker. Drawings of c. 1805 in the Murray Collection (now in the National Library) and signed "Gandon &
Baker" show that the whole design and composition had then
been determined (138), while an elevation of 1815 signed by
Francis Johnston shows that his contribution consisted only
of a few swags and decorative flourishes. The buildings were
finished by 1817.

8

Descending Constitution Hill, whose Irish name was Glasmanoge, we have on our left the site of the old Linen Hall, destroyed in the troubles, and on our right a series of large hospitals and institutional buildings, mostly designed by Francis Johnston. They include the House of Industry (1806–19), now the Legion of Mary Hostels, in which William Murray collaborated, and the Richmond Penitentiary (1810–12) and Richmond Lunatic Asylum (1814–17), both now parts of Grangegorman Asylum. The narrow opening of Church Street continues the way down to the foot of the old bridge, which in spite of its many official names is commonly called Church Street Bridge; here on our left is the Public Record Office in the enclosure of the Four Courts. Shortly before reaching the back of the Four Courts, and on the other, west side of the street, is the old church and churchyard of St. Michan's. The "ch" is pronounced hard, as in Michael. The church has a fine battlemented tower of the usual Irish type, evidently from the late middle ages, though standing on the site of a Danish church said to have been built in 1096 (157). There was an extensive restoration or rebuilding in 1686, when the baroque west doorway was inserted, and most of the present church goes back only to an even more drastic work of 1828. There is, however, exceedingly fine woodwork inside, and an organ dated 1724, with an elaborate carved console of musical instruments in high relief. This organ was made by Cuvillie, and the statement is often made that it is the one on which Handel played in 1742. But according to the researches of Mr. W. F. Wakeman in 1887, Handel's organ had been at the Blue-Coat School twenty years before that time, and subsequently at Isaac Butt's house in Eccles Street, while the St. Michan's instrument could be proved to have been in the church ever since it was built.

St. Michan's is notorious for its vaults cut from the magnesian limestone, which is so absorbent as to prevent decomposition and to cause an unusual form of soft mummification. The appearance of the bodies so preserved is said not to be "really gruesome", but photographs hardly suggest that a visit can increase the jollity of the day's proceedings. Whether it is right to permit public access to sights of a shocking and horrifying character is a much disputed point, and I do not propose to enter upon it here. But what is objectionable at St. Michan's is that the visit to the vaults has been made a

83　Within the Catholic Pro-Cathedral

84　Statue of Our Lady of Dublin, early 16th century. Said to have been saved from the wreck of St. Mary's Abbey at the Dissolution, and now in the Church of the Calced Carmelites, Whitefriar Street

85   In O'Connell Street

86   On the Grand Canal

DUBLIN TRANSPORT

highly publicized function for tourists, from which the (Church of Ireland) parish derives a large revenue. Such exploitation of the private dead is even more disgraceful than the filthy state of desecration which is the lot of many of the older graveyards of Ireland. It is hard to understand the insensitive mentality of the ghouls who carry on this lucrative show.

Behind St. Michan's churchyard is the broad expanse of Smithfield, and a little farther on the charming little piece of town-planning at Blackhall Street (1789) and Blackhall Place, in front of Thomas Ivory's Blue-Coat School (8). The school's official name is the King's Hospital, and as a foundation by Royal Charter of Charles II in 1672, the choir boys still wear scarlet cassocks, though the old blue uniform was abolished as an inconvenience in 1923. Ivory's original design proved to be too costly, and the committee meeting which he attended to discuss cutting down of expenditure is commemorated by a contemporary painting by John Trotter in the board-room. The board-room is also of interest for the fine design of its plaster ceiling, made for £72 in 1778–80 by Charles Thorp the elder. The present work is an exact reproduction, the original having been wrecked not long ago by an accidental fire. The buildings, begun in 1773, came to a standstill ten years later, and the tall central cupola, the drawings for which have been preserved, remained for a hundred and fifty years unfinished. In the present century (1904) it has been brought to an unsatisfactory makeshift conclusion by the removal of the unfinished work and substitution of a sort of pepper-pot.

Concluding our view of Dublin, we may glance at the turning out of the top of Blackhall Place, which bears the unusual name of Stoneybatter. This is more logical than it looks, for it is a mongrel composed of the English "stony" and the Irish *bóthar*, "a road". More to the purpose, this was probably the earliest of roads into Dublin, for Dr. George Little considers this a part of the *Slighe Cualann*, that one of the five grand highways from Tara which led southwards to Cualu, the land of south Dublin and the present County Wicklow. Future scientific excavation of the line between Blackhall Place and Father Mathew Bridge may prove this hypothesis, but at least we know that in walking along Stoneybatter we form part of an innumerable concourse who for untold centuries, strangers and Irish, have trodden the road to and from Dublin.

IV

The Surroundings of Dublin

BEFORE ATTEMPTING TO DESCRIBE DUBLIN'S DEVELOPMENT, this seems a suitable point for looking at the environs in which Dublin is set. Those who require details are referred to the admirable book: *The Neighbourhood of Dublin*, by Mr. Weston St. John Joyce. Here we shall consider not the details, but the general picture of the surrounding country, and as much of its history as is essential to an understanding of the city.

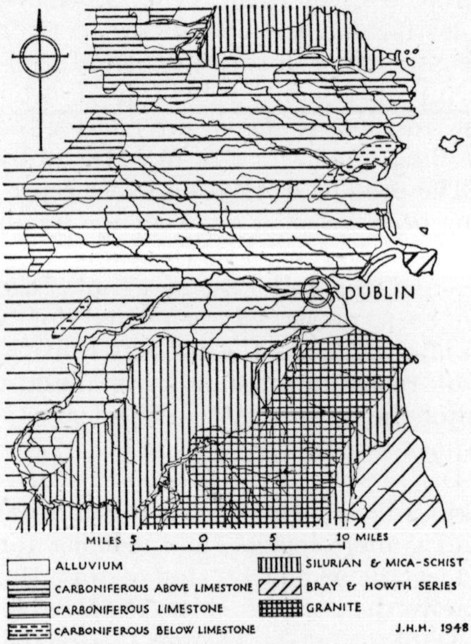

Dublin lies at the focal point of a great field of carboniferous limestone, through which several rivers have cut shallow valleys falling into the Bay (**107**). Chief of these is the Liffey, true source of Dublin, which rises on the granite range of the Wicklow Mountains and taking in the King's River and other tributaries cuts across the Silurian belt to the limestone. The limestone shelf, sloping upwards to the interior, changes the river's direction, and henceforth it follows at a slight distance the dipping edge of the silurian strata. Further small streams flow in on both sides, most important the Rye Water at Leixlip, just below the shelf forming the salmon leap which gives the village its Norse name. From Leixlip the river flows almost due eastward in a slightly undulating line to the sea.

87 Geology of the Dublin region

MILES 5 0 5 10 MILES

ALLUVIUM
CARBONIFEROUS ABOVE LIMESTONE
CARBONIFEROUS LIMESTONE
CARBONIFEROUS BELOW LIMESTONE
SILURIAN & MICA-SCHIST
BRAY & HOWTH SERIES
GRANITE

J.H.H. 1948

DUBLIN

60

A few miles to the North, the Tolka comes down the limestone from the direction of Tara, its valley followed by the *Slighe Cualann*, as represented by the modern main road through Clonee and Dunshaughlin. On the south comes the Dodder, straight down from the Dublin granite, and between the Dodder and the Liffey lie the smaller streams of the Poddle and the Cammock, which discharge into the Liffey in Dublin.

All these waters bring down great quantities of alluvium, and the fact that the Tolka and the Dodder enter the bay more or less in line, but of course in opposite directions, assisted the building up of a bar across the mouth of the Liffey, and consequently the growth of a safe river-port within.

Now while the relative positions of the three rivers settled the fate of Dublin as a harbour, it was more especially the course of the Dodder which made possible its emergence

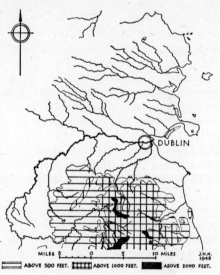

88 Contours and rivers of the Dublin region

as a great town. For the most vital factor in any large assembly of human beings is water-supply. The Tolka, flowing entirely on the limestone, and deprived of mountain sources, has normally but a slight volume, and the flooded Liffey is undesirable as drinking water on account of the dark product of the bogs which enters it copiously on its long course of twenty miles from Kilcullen to Celbridge. The Dodder, on the other hand, brings fresh mountain water down in spate at all seasons, for the slopes of mighty Kippure are never without rainfall (**88**). From very early times to the present day, it has been the heavy rainfall on this southern mountain mass that has made Dublin possible, just as it has been the suddenly contrasting dryness of the riverine climate that has given Dublin its own character. Ever since the thirteenth century, when the inhabitants produced a main water supply by diverting a part of the Dodder into the Poddle, and then taking a portion of the combined flow into an artificial channel, the provision of increasing supplies, adequate to the growing population, has been a first charge on the forethought of the city's governors.

The significance of Dublin grows out of a number of pairs of factors, each pair acting as generators of some aspect of its life. Thus we have the rivers with their alluvial load on the one hand, and the sea on the other, going to produce a safe port, the juxtaposition of a dry place to dwell in, and a wet one to provide drinking water; the natives inland, and the strangers from the sea, meeting to transact business. Similarly the position of Dublin on a political frontier had great significance: there has, quite apart from Ireland's struggles against the outsider, been a perpetual if often silent warfare between the forces of the North and of the South. What is the modern North County came within the grasp of the High King seated at Tara, an appanage of Royal Meath; but beyond the Liffey was a country always within easy reach of the wild men who lived in the high hills of Cualu, a country that was not to be subdued to any form of civilized life until the nineteenth century. Yet this wild country of barbarians was in early times a place of particular consequence as a principal source of gold. From this native gold, small quantities of which are still washed from the Wicklow stream beds, were made the magnificent ornaments that graced the courts of ancient Ireland, and still attract the excited attention of the visitor to the National Museum. So here again we can see the importance of the Dublin river-crossing in the internal trade of Ireland between the gold-producing region of Wicklow, and the gold-demanding regions across the Liffey in the fertile midlands—even more important was the external effect of Ireland's export of gold and gold ornaments, and other metallic products, to Western Europe even as early as the second millenium B.C. As Dr. Adolf Mahr has expressed it: Wicklow was then the country of El Dorado.

The modern County Dublin is then an artificial formation expressing the expansive force of the city's inhabitants: it is made up of two quite diverse territories—the flat coastal plain north of Dublin, still known as Fingal from the *Gall* or foreigners who settled in it, and the essential minimum strip

A few miles to the North, the Tolka comes down the limestone from the direction of Tara, its valley followed by the *Slighe Cualann*, as represented by the modern main road through Clonee and Dunshaughlin. On the south comes the Dodder, straight down from the Dublin granite, and between the Dodder and the Liffey lie the smaller streams of the Poddle and the Cammock, which discharge into the Liffey in Dublin.

All these waters bring down great quantities of alluvium, and the fact that the Tolka and the Dodder enter the bay more or less in line, but of course in opposite directions, assisted the building up of a bar across the mouth of the Liffey, and consequently the growth of a safe river-port within.

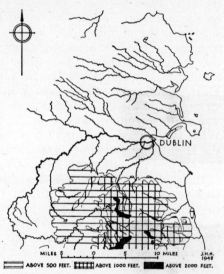

MILES 5 0 5 10 MILES J.H.H. 1948
ABOVE 500 FEET. ABOVE 1000 FEET. ABOVE 2000 FEET.

88 Contours and rivers of the Dublin region

Now while the relative positions of the three rivers settled the fate of Dublin as a harbour, it was more especially the course of the Dodder which made possible its emergence as a great town. For the most vital factor in any large assembly of human beings is water-supply. The Tolka, flowing entirely on the limestone, and deprived of mountain sources, has normally but a slight volume, and the flooded Liffey is undesirable as drinking water on account of the dark product of the bogs which enters it copiously on its long course of twenty miles from Kilcullen to Celbridge. The Dodder, on the other hand, brings fresh mountain water down in spate at all seasons, for the slopes of mighty Kippure are never without rainfall (**88**). From very early times to the present day, it has been the heavy rainfall on this southern mountain mass that has made Dublin possible, just as it has been the suddenly contrasting dryness of the riverine climate that has given Dublin its own character. Ever since the thirteenth century, when the inhabitants produced a main water supply by diverting a part of the Dodder into the Poddle, and then taking a portion of the combined flow into an artificial channel, the provision of increasing supplies, adequate to the growing population, has been a first charge on the forethought of the city's governors.

The significance of Dublin grows out of a number of pairs of factors, each pair acting as generators of some aspect of its life. Thus we have the rivers with their alluvial load on the one hand, and the sea on the other, going to produce a safe port, the juxtaposition of a dry place to dwell in, and a wet one to provide drinking water; the natives inland, and the strangers from the sea, meeting to transact business. Similarly the position of Dublin on a political frontier had great significance: there has, quite apart from Ireland's struggles against the outsider, been a perpetual if often silent warfare between the forces of the North and of the South. What is the modern North County came within the grasp of the High King seated at Tara, an appanage of Royal Meath; but beyond the Liffey was a country always within easy reach of the wild men who lived in the high hills of Cualu, a country that was not to be subdued to any form of civilized life until the nineteenth century. Yet this wild country of barbarians was in early times a place of particular consequence as a principal source of gold. From this native gold, small quantities of which are still washed from the Wicklow stream beds, were made the magnificent ornaments that graced the courts of ancient Ireland, and still attract the excited attention of the visitor to the National Museum. So here again we can see the importance of the Dublin river-crossing in the internal trade of Ireland between the gold-producing region of Wicklow, and the gold-demanding regions across the Liffey in the fertile midlands—even more important was the external effect of Ireland's export of gold and gold ornaments, and other metallic products, to Western Europe even as early as the second millenium B.C. As Dr. Adolf Mahr has expressed it: Wicklow was then the country of El Dorado.

The modern County Dublin is then an artificial formation expressing the expansive force of the city's inhabitants: it is made up of two quite diverse territories—the flat coastal plain north of Dublin, still known as Fingal from the *Gall* or foreigners who settled in it, and the essential minimum strip

89   The City Hall, formerly the Royal Exchange, 1769–79
Thomas Cooley, architect
From a colour-print by S. F. Brocas, 1830

90   St. Catherine's Church, Thomas Street, 1760–9
John Smith, architect
From the aquatint by James Malton

91   THE MAIN FRONT OF TRINITY COLLEGE, 1752-60.   Henry Keene and John Sanderson, architects

From a print by Thomas Malton, 1797

of Cualu on the south, for some centuries past referred to as Merrion. How far back this welding of a pair of diverse halves into a single territorial unit goes is uncertain. The County Dublin at any rate goes back to the time of King John, but it may be that the Bristol colonists who consolidated English power in the city merely took over a shadowy pre-existing territory of the Vikings, for the Norse kingdom of Dublin certainly stretched down the coast, although under the nominal suzerainty of the King of Leinster. There is even a probable connexion with the substratum of native Irish land tenure and land division.

This is a complicated and obscure subject, and Professor James Hogan has pointed out that even as early as the beginning of the historical period in Ireland, there were two overlapping systems of land-division, where in theory only one would be expected. Ideally the country was divided into a settled number of "Tuaths" or political units, and each of these units subdivided for purposes of taxation into a number of "Bailes" or towns, with the further divisions, in descending order, of half-Baile, Quarter, half-Quarter, and Ploughland. But in fact, often independently of the division of the actual Tuaths, there was a series of fiscal units, each known as a "Tricha cét", and subdivided into 30 Baile Biataighs, each comprising 12 ploughlands of 120 acres of arable land each. One of the most interesting points is that the name Baile Biataigh means Victualler's Town, and records the early custom of having a public refectory or hostel in each Baile. This again links up with the state of affairs in Saxon England, where Walter Map records that there were drinking-houses, one in each parish, called in English *ghildhus*.

These early fiscal units are sometimes represented by the rural deaneries of the ancient dioceses, just as the sees themselves have the boundaries of the old kingdoms; sometimes too the tuaths have become the civil baronies into which the counties of Ireland are still divided. It is necessary to say a few words here about the historical and modern system of land administration in Ireland, in so far as it differs in fact or in nomenclature from English practice. The English division was and is into counties, and each county used to be divided into hundreds, each of which in theory represented 100 free families, each family supported by a hide of land of 120 acres. A community of ten freemen with their families formed a tithing, which might or might not be a parish of itself. Many parishes included a large number of tithings, until they were split up in modern times—the normal test of the parish was that it was the area whose tithes contributed to the support of a priest; and here we get again the confusion between civil and religious boundaries. Roughly it would seem that there is a correspondence between the English tithing (or township in the north of England) and the Irish townland; between parish and parish; between hundred and barony; and between county and county. But one must beware of too exact equation.

Taking Ireland as a whole and comparing it with England as a whole, there is one very great and outstanding difference between the two types of agricultural economy. In England, as opposed to Ireland and also to Wales and Cornwall, the norm is the nucleated village composed of a group of farmhouses, each acting as head of an estate large or small and scattered or compact, but in any case spread out in the countryside about the village. In Ireland and the other Celtic lands, on the contrary, the houses themselves are scattered broadcast, and true villages are non-existent. Look for example at the half-inch scale map of Newry: from Dundalk to Portadown and all over the backland of the Mourne Mountains there are thousands of isolated dots representing houses, and hundreds upon hundreds of little lanes forming a labyrinthine web; contrast with this a similar map of midland or eastern England, which will show a nucleated village every two or three miles, comparatively few roads, and bare tracts of open country in between. But, and this is the striking thing, the maps of the Dublin area show an "English" and not an Irish layout.

The reason of this discrepancy is obvious: the County Dublin and considerable parts of the adjoining counties were largely anglicized through seven centuries, and even before that had been partially settled by the strangers, the Danish and Norse Vikings of the kingdom of Dublin. There is another piece of evidence which shows the extent of this anglicization even more clearly: the prevalence in the Dublin area of traces of the open field system of arable cultivation. It is now a commonplace that until a century or so ago the greater part of England consisted of village communities possessing open unfenced fields of great size, in which the inhabitants possessed scattered strips of land, up and down the fields, hither and thither. Each man was dependent on his neighbour for co-operative cultivation, yet each man was the permanent possessor of his own separate strips. Dr. and Mrs. Orwin in their classic book on *The Open Fields* have shown that this system or modifications of it was once prevalent over the whole of England, with the exception of Cumbria, Lancashire, Cheshire, Devon and Cornwall; Wales also has no traces of it. It is true that in the Celtic countries a system known as runrig or rundale operated, but in this the strips were constantly

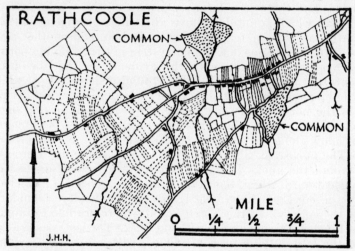

92 Rathcoole, Co. Dublin, *c.* 1825, to show arable land in strips

subjected to redistribution; that is, there was no permanent ownership of the separate strips. Both Saxon and Danish England and its Celtic neighbours had communal methods of cultivation; but the English insisted on the permanent and hereditary transmission of each individual piece of land.

There must be an immense volume of evidence bearing upon this question, but I will give two instances. Some eighteenth century rentals of the Earl of Shelburne's estates were printed in 1939 by the late Alderman Thomas Kelly. In 1757 the Manor of Drimnagh (3 miles south-west of Dublin) included "a stripe adjoyning Mr. Dillon's holding", while in Clondalkin (another mile or so to the west) there was "a piece called the 3 Stangs", and "two stripes near Garranstown". Now it is true that these stripes or strips might have

belonged to a runrig system, but this is quite impossible in
the case of the lands of Rathcoole, of which a large number of
plans exist, showing a permanent division of properties comprised of strips. These maps have recently been the subject of
a valuable series of notes by Mr. Liam Ua Broin, who does
not, however, discuss the evidence of open-field cultivation.
But the maps themselves are speaking witnesses that the
strips existed from before 1670 until 1826 or later. Most of
the maps show some one holding of scattered strips in the
fields, but there is a large-scale map of the whole area of
c. 1825 which admirably shows the whole arrangement (**92**).
Rathcoole is some ten miles out of Dublin, and another map
of 1816 shows signs of a similar system in the adjoining parish
of Saggart. Agreeing with the evidence of the Shelburne
rentals, a map of Clondalkin in 1746 also shows strips, while
a later plan of *c.* 1782 shows the system in advanced decay.
On the north of the city, strips are perhaps indicated on a
plan of Glasnevin, but these are possibly strips of common
meadow along the valley of the Tolka.

The nucleated village is also very well represented around
Dublin: the above instances of open fields are also cases of
nucleation; Rathfarnham (**97**) is another good instance close
to the city, and Newcastle Lyons on the Kildare boundary
of the county. In the North County there are fine examples
at Finglas, Glasnevin, Swords, and Lusk. The last is as typical
of the labyrinthine form of village, with repeatedly looping
back-lanes, as are Bloxham or Wroxton in North Oxfordshire.
Of Lusk an extremely valuable survey was made in 1943
by the Material Culture Survey Group of the Dublin University College School of Architecture, under Mr. M. Mac-
Dermot; the village map, and sheets of plans, elevations and
sections of individual cottages, are on exhibition in the
National Museum. Another factor which tended to approxi-
mation between the County Dublin village and its English
prototype was the manorial system of overlordship, complete
with courts leet and courts baron, stewards and village officers,
which was certainly transplanted to Ireland, but which has left
far less copious traces in the form of documents than might
have been expected. During the Middle Ages there were also
the church and monastic estates, of very large extent around
Dublin, and these were administered on lines laid down by the
practice of English mother houses such as Buildwas Abbey.

93–5 The single-storey terrace, a peculiarity of the southern suburbs of Dublin, c. 1830–60

96   Kenilworth Square, Rathgar

97   Rathfarnham Village

These then were some of the factors which helped to determine the course of Dublin's development during the centuries following the English invasion. A colony of Bristol, Dublin more closely resembles the great West Country port than any other English city, though its peculiar conditions, subject to attack by the natives, suggest Chester, Shrewsbury or Hereford as the nearest counterparts, while its position in several important respects is like that of London itself. It has even acquired the singular superstitions of a great capital from London, if we may trust James Joyce. Joyce says that you never cross O'Connell Bridge without meeting a white horse; but this is notably a London Bridge superstition. It is rather an amusing speculation to consider the circumstances in which the white horses may have been notified of the necessity to change their venue from the Old Bridge to Essex Bridge, or from Essex to Carlisle Bridge. At any rate, the white horse is a Saxon and Jutish emblem.

The distribution of the old civil parishes within the county is strangely irregular; enormous parishes like Tallaght and Lusk jostle those of normal size such as Rathfarnham and Finglas, and minuscules of the size of Kilmahuddrick and Killester (**98**). As in England, it is evident that there must have been a good deal of adjustment to suit the ecclesiastical and lay owners of estates, and the same phenomenon appears that was once so common in England, of divided parishes with isolated enclaves belonging to them elsewhere, just as Llivia, belonging to Spain, is entirely surrounded by French territory. But in Ireland there is a notable difference regarding the system of townlands. The English tithings and townships often had no distinct boundaries; Irish townlands, on the other hand, are the one permanent feature of the whole series of land-divisions: county boundaries have changed greatly, civil parishes have been abolished, but the townland still remains an unchanged unit. The reason is that it is a relic of the native Irish system which covered the countryside before parishes and counties were thought of; split townlands occur, divided between separate parishes. Clearly the mesh of smaller units was in existence before the lines of the parishes were superimposed.

As elsewhere in the Middle Ages, jurisdictions were many and conflicting. Not only was the country parcelled out into lay and church baronies and manors, but as those in lay hands

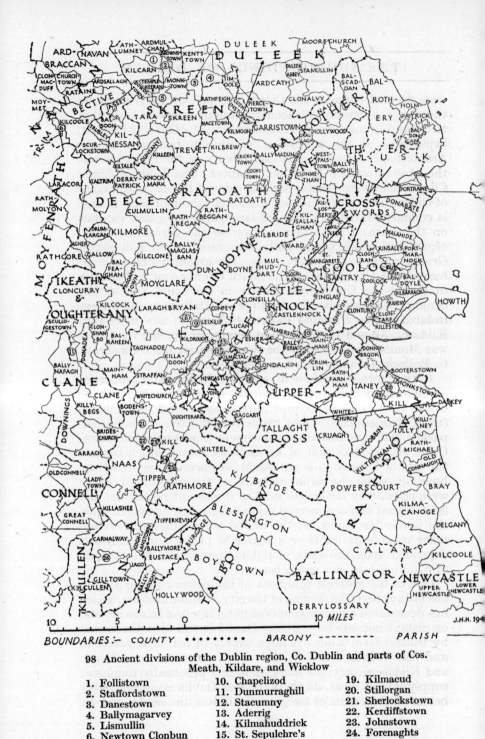

98 Ancient divisions of the Dublin region, Co. Dublin and parts of Cos.
Meath, Kildare, and Wicklow

1. Follistown
2. Staffordstown
3. Danestown
4. Ballymagarvey
5. Lismullin
6. Newtown Clonbun
7. Killegland
8. Donaghmore
9. Kilmacredock
10. Chapelizod
11. Dunmurraghill
12. Stacumny
13. Aderrig
14. Kilmahuddrick
15. St. Sepulchre's
16. Castledillon
17. Clonaghlis
18. Kilbride
19. Kilmacud
20. Stillorgan
21. Sherlockstown
22. Kerdiffstown
23. Johnstown
24. Forenaghts
25. Haynestown
26. Brannockstown

were divided between the Crown and private individuals, so those of the church belonged to various religious bodies, or to separate functions of the same church—the Liberty of St. Sepulchre's in the south-east of Dublin belonged to the Archbishop, while the adjacent Liberty of St. Patrick's was the precinct of the Dean and Chapter. The Prior of Christ Church held great estates on both sides of the city: the manor of Glasnevin and Gorman on the north (the monastic grange is commemorated in the name Grangegorman), and Clonken on the south, a great manor covering the parishes of Still-organ, Kill, Killiney and Tully; the present name Kill-of-the-Grange refers to the priory farm. The archbishopric held the baronies of Uppercross in the South County and Nethercross in Fingal—to Uppercross, mostly in the south-west of the county, belonged also the vital port of Dalkey, as did a large isolated territory around Ballymore Eustace, now in County Kildare. Among the important estates of St. Mary's Abbey was Monkstown, covering the whole district from Blackrock to Bullock, through Dun Laoghaire.

In their own ways these diverse jurisdictions and properties all influenced the story of Dublin, for craftsmen might be drawn to work in an exempt liberty, and rich demesne lands (as at Kilmainham) might prove so attractive as to be em-parked and thus prevent expansion in a particular direction. Other estates, like that of All Hallows Priory which became the site of Trinity College, would be partially secured from building, while the adjacent lands of the nuns of St. Mary were intensively developed into an important residential and later official and commercial centre. So much depended upon the particular owner, at the period when building develop-ment became desirable or a source of profit; and much also depended upon the state of public opinion and the theories of planning held at a given time.

One of the greatest functions of the district round Dublin has always been the feeding of the city. Unlike London, which has devastated a vast region of countryside and has to depend on distant imports for a living, Dublin is still interpenetrated by fruitful farm lands. A large supply of fish is available in and just outside the Bay, and the broad pastures of Meath and Kildare supply the markets with a practically unlimited supply of fresh meat. In these respects Dublin is incomparably better off than most of the great capitals of the world, and she is still more so in the relative purity of her air, and in the fact that the hills and open country can be seen from many points of vantage throughout the city. The citizens are fortunate again in the number of pleasure resorts and places of scenic beauty within easy reach.

There are two kinds of open space available for public recreation: the last few generations have seen wide recognition of the need of city populations for parks and accessible stretches of fields and woods, partly for the sake of exercise in clean air, partly for repose in green and pleasant surroundings. The rather negative good qualities of such open spaces are typified by the London parks and by St. Stephen's Green (**114**) and the People's Garden of Dublin. But the second and far more valuable sort of recreation depends upon another factor: positive physical beauty of the place itself and of the view. These requirements are fulfilled repeatedly in the immediate neighbourhood of Dublin. For a few pence the jaded worker can reach the sea breezes and magnificent scenery of Howth or Killiney, or from Rathfarnham or Bohernabreena climb into the high hills, still almost primaeval in their untouched splendour. Even the destitute can see the blue sparkling waters of the Bay and enjoy the prospect from the Phoenix Park. Not London, nor Paris nor even Vienna can show comparable riches of encircling beauty.

In the eighteenth century Dublin set an artificial check upon her growth by making the North and South Circular Roads and accepting the area enclosed as a final limit. Just beyond this limit the two great canals were built, so that for several generations the growth of housing was held in by a ring fence. This roughly corresponded with the ancient jurisdiction of the city, and it is only in the last few years that the new urban developments beyond this line have all (apart from Dun Laoghaire) been brought within a greater Dublin. To a certain degree, the lack of a concerted plan implied by this long-standing division has been unfortunate. The outskirts of Dublin are rather more incoherent than they need have been, and a good deal of money has been wasted upon separate and overlapping services of various kinds: water supply, public libraries and the like. But whether inside or outside the city, there is an intense local patriotism of the suburbs which has preserved the precious spark of individuality so generally lost elsewhere.

To live within the old boundaries of the city is now generally

101 Doorway, No. 38 Fitzwilliam
Street, *c.* 1800

102   Doorway, No. 16 Upper
Merrion Street, 1778

103   No. 42   104   No. 40
Doorways in Dominick Street, *c.* 1760

99 Upper Mount Street, looking towards St. Stephen's Church, 1824-5
J. Bowden, architect

100 Merrion Square: north side, 1762-4
John Ensor and George Ensor, architects

the lot only of the very rich or the very poor—and always speaking relatively, it must be remembered that there are few very rich people in the whole of Eire. There is only the one well-to-do section left in the city, the south-eastern quarter beyond St. Stephen's Green, consisting of Merrion and Fitzwilliam Squares, and the streets immediately adjacent to and connecting them. West of this lies the important business district of Dawson, Grafton, and Dame Streets, the commercial and banking district near the river, and the big shops and hotels of O'Connell Street. All the rest ranges from decent but impoverished shopping quarters down to slums. The suburbs proper can be divided into north and south, and these again into inner and outer, lying on the hither or farther sides of the Tolka and Dodder respectively.

The principal inner suburbs are Cabra and Drumcondra on the northern side, and a much larger range on the south: Ballsbridge, Donnybrook, Milltown, Rathmines, Rathgar (**96**), Harolds Cross, Terenure, Kimmage and Crumlin. Beyond the Tolka are Glasnevin, Marino, Clontarf and Raheny, and a series of dormitory towns along the coast towards Drogheda—Baldoyle, Malahide, Rush, Skerries and Balbriggan. The southern counterparts are Sandymount, Dundrum (pronounced Dun-drum, with accent on the second syllable), Rathfarnham (**97**), with coastal townships at Blackrock, Dun Laoghaire (**94**), Dalkey, Killiney (**107**), Bray and Greystones, and inland districts of purely dormitory type at Stillorgan, Foxrock and Carrickmines. Of all these places, Glasnevin, Rathfarnham, Dundrum and Dalkey still retain vestiges of their older life as villages or small towns; Bray is a great seaside resort, often termed the Brighton of Ireland, but still preserving its old countrified main street, running uphill. The southern belt from Sandymount to Terenure was developed in the mid-nineteenth century, in the afterglow of Dublin's classic age, and so were Blackrock and Kingstown. Consequently there are many charming small houses in these districts, sometimes of brick but often stucco-fronted (**93–5**). They are in style what would be called Regency in England, but they generally date from 1830 to 1860. Kenilworth Square, Rathgar (**96**), is the most notable expression of planning in the suburban belt, while there is an elaborate example of modern "garden-planning" at Marino, on the lands of the old Charlemont estate. Of the eighteenth-century magnificence of Marino, only Chambers' exquisite little Casino is left, a nymph forlorn among the Christian Brothers' playing fields beside the red-brick O'Brien's Institute (**105**).

Howth is chiefly important for its glorious views and the fauna and flora of its cliffs, but the deserted harbour that might have been the gateway of Ireland is picturesque, and there are extensive remains of the ruined Abbey. Howth Castle was built in 1564, but greatly altered at various later dates. Its gardens, and especially the Rhododendron Walk, are deservedly famous, and impressive even to those who, like myself, have no love for the rhododendron as a flower. The estate passed in the male line of the one family from the time of the Conquest of Ireland until, within living memory, the Earldom of Howth became extinct. Almeric or Amory Tristram, one of Strongbow's followers, drove out from Howth the Danes who had taken refuge there after the fall of Dublin, and winning the victory upon St. Lawrence's Day, took the saint's name as his own. There is at the castle a very ancient tree, said to drop a limb for the death of every male of the house of St. Lawrence.

Opposite Howth on the south shore of the Bay is Kingstown Harbour, Howth's successor as a packet station for England, and one of the greatest ports of refuge in the British Isles. Until the eighteenth century Dunleary was a mere fishing hamlet in the parish of Monkstown, then began to share in the new fashion of seaside watering places, and about 1760 provided itself with a new, now the Old, Pier. A plan of 1770 shows the parish of Monkstown still almost wholly open country, while a larger and more detailed survey a generation later indicates the growing settlement at Salt Hill and the provision, discreetly separated by a reef of rocks, of "Men's Bathing Place" and "Women's Bathing Place", where the base of the West Pier now stands. The East Pier was the first portion of the great harbour to be built, between 1817 and 1821, but the harbour was not fully completed until 1859. George IV, on his visit of 1821, landed at Howth and left from Dunleary, renamed Kingstown in his honour. A curious obelisk supported on four stone cannon-balls and surmounted by a well-upholstered crown still commemorates the royal departure.

The tale of the Dublin & Kingstown Railway, Ireland's first and most profitable line, has been told in detail by Mr. Kevin Murray, from whose valuable papers I borrow the salient

105, 106 The Casino, Marino, Clontarf,
1757–71. Sir William Chambers, architect

107   Killiney Bay, with Bray Head and the Sugarloaf Mountains

points. Begun in 1832, the first train was drawn by horses on the 31st of July, 1834, locomotives arrived in October, and the line from Westland Row to the foot of Kingstown West Pier was opened to the public on the 17th of December (38). The inhabitants of Kingstown at first refused to have the smoking monster brought nearer to their doors, but soon capitulated, and William Dargan, the great contractor, rapidly pushed the line on in 1836–7 to the site of the present Dun Laoghaire Station; the extension was opened on the 17th of May, 1837, but the present station buildings, with their elegant classic offices (20) and great terminal train-shed (now bereft of its roof) only date from 1854. The present through platform represents the starting point of the atmospheric railway to Dalkey, begun in 1842 and built by Dargan. The new line was complete by August 1843, but not publicly opened until the 29th March, 1844; it cost £38,000, and was worked as a separate undertaking on the atmospheric principle until the 12th of April 1854, when through working by steam began. Both the Dublin & Kingstown and Dalkey railways were built to the standard English gauge of 4 ft. 8½ in., but when they were leased by the Dublin & Wicklow Railway in 1856 and connected with its main line near Bray, they were converted to the Irish standard of 5 ft. 3 in.

The extension of the railway from Dalkey which connects with the Wicklow main line, and that line itself, run through some of the finest scenery in Ireland. Between Dalkey and Killiney stations the seaward carriage windows frame the glorious view of Killiney Bay (107), closed by the two Sugarloaf mountains and Bray Head in the distance. Beyond Killiney the first line ran almost along the shore, but has had to be rebuilt some distance inland owing to coastal erosion, and a similar fate has overtaken the earlier alignments round the dizzy cliffs of Bray Head. Above the railway from Dalkey runs the scenic Vico Road, on which scores of motor-cars are parked on summer weekends; the Irish certainly cannot be accused of lack of appreciation of their own beauty-spots, which are indeed overrun except in working hours. Those who cannot afford a trip to Killiney or Howth flock to the beaches between Sandymount and Salt Hill and swim and sunbathe in their thousands. Fortunate Dubliners, with endless store of sunlight and sea water and fresh air on your doorsteps—may you make the most of your blessings, and never lose them!

V
The Growth of Dublin

THIS IS NOT A HISTORY, AND I HAVE TRIED TO AVOID AS FAR as possible the anecdotal aspect of Dublin, for this has received such full treatment at the hands of acknowledged masters of the pen. The Irish capital has indeed provoked a rich harvest of fine writing, and for living pictures of a highly personal culture, what city can show a literary sunburst equal to the combined effect of W. B. Yeats's *Autobiographies*, George Moore's *Hail and Farewell*, J. M. Synge's prose essays, the works of James Joyce, plays of Sean O'Casey, and Dr. Gogarty's *Sackville Street*? I would mention two other books dealing with the events of the last generation in Dublin: Mr. P. L. Dickinson's admirable impressions of *The Dublin of Yesterday*, and "An Englishman's" *Dublin Explorations and Reflections* of 1917, an extraordinarily detached and very thorough picture of the state of affairs immediately after the rebellion of Easter Week. As *Hail and Farewell* stands head and shoulders above the rest as a work of pure literature, so does this author's shrewd and witty thumbnail sketch of a crucial period excel all the guide-books to Dublin ever written.

An outstanding section of the book discusses and contrasts the English and Irish mentalities in the war of 1914; I must quote one passage which is as true to-day as it was thirty years ago. "In Dublin" says "An Englishman", "one feels that men's thoughts are really *free*. I don't believe any Irishman could tolerate for an instant the kind of claptrap which in England does duty for opinions. Prejudices probably exist in Dublin, just as much as they do in London, but they are of a different nature and they are not so childishly absurd, not so absolutely destructive of any and every form of ratiocination. To the Liberty-loving Englishman one of the most noticeable and pleasant things about Dublin is that it is a veritable stronghold of Liberty—perhaps one of the very few such strongholds left in Europe." He continues, horrifyingly but accurately: "The descendants of the men who gave their lives in order to induce Liberty to abide with them have now turned round and kicked her out of doors. She has fallen down that well into which Militarism has already chucked the bayoneted bodies of Justice and Truth. In Ireland the stranger feels that no such disaster could possibly befall the community. There freedom may be attacked from without, but it is not (as is the case with England) attacked from within".

Early in this book I stressed the importance of environment in producing the qualities we associate with Dublin, and this is nowhere better seen than in connexion with Dublin freedom of mind and ready wit. Even immigrants of middle age acquire the Dublin spirit. For example, James Gandon was visiting the works of his new Corinthian portico at the Parliament House in 1785, when he was stopped by a stranger who asked him what the order of the columns was, seeing that they differed from those of the Ionic colonnade in front. Gandon gave him the typically Dublin answer: "Sir, the order you are now enquiring about is a very substantial one, being an order of the House of Lords". It would be a great advantage to England if residence for three to five years in Dublin were part of a complete education.

The twentieth century in Dublin is overshadowed by The Troubles, which bulk larger than the Literary Revival that made Irish independence a possibility. There were of course many points of close contact between the Revival and the Rebels—Patrick Pearse and Thomas MacDonagh were poets, and MacDonagh in particular was associated with Edward Martyn in his theatrical venture. But the heroes died, leaving the politicians behind, and it cannot be said that the politicians saw with the same eyes as did the leaders of the great artistic movement: one has only to consider the imposition of a censorship of a crassly stupid sort, in the teeth of the opposition of W. B. Yeats and what was left of the band of singers.

The troubles threw up one great and grand figure, whose memory still broods over the Irish State: Michael Collins (19). He was in every sense big; even filtered down and diminished through the telescope of twenty-five years his career is on an epic scale; his exploits and ultimate death compare with those of Du Guesclin in the Hundred Years War or of Rommel in that just ended. Collins had the magic touch which captured the imagination and won the respect even of stern opponents, and the mind stubbornly kicks against the bitter fact that such men seem never to be spared to complete the work they have begun. Lavery's deathbed portrait of Collins in the Municipal Gallery, entitled "Love for Ireland", has a value far beyond most of that painter's work, for it is illumined and transmuted by the grandeur and the tragedy of Collins' dead body. One can fancy that in some countries the head of Collins would have been carved to titanic scale on some mountain side, that the features of the founder of New Ireland might last as long as Time itself.

Dublin has produced an extraordinary number of "characters": men whose individuality combined greatness with eccentricity. In the generation before Collins the outstanding character was Sir John Pentland Mahaffy, at the end of his life Provost of Trinity (**111**). There is a certain species of joke or pawky story which is particularly common in Dublin; not necessarily brilliant as wit, but good enough to be worth passing on. Of recent years such stories have perhaps tended to centre round Dr. Gogarty, but still by far the majority are told of Mahaffy. He was the most overwhelming personality of the Dublin that knew liberal Viceroys, Ulster agitation, and the opening of the Great War—and he is still thought of as the greatest character living men have known. In other words, something of the veneration and modified alarm that is felt in London about Mr. Bernard Shaw (another Dubliner) is felt, much more intimately, about Mahaffy in Dublin. He was a man of wide and deep learning, evidently one of the rudest men that ever lived, and yet representing a quality which people of all ranks and views could respect. For a very long time to come Mahaffy-stories will circulate, but when at length they die out his memory will be perpetuated by the work of his Georgian Society, which only just in time gathered together almost everything that needed to be known about Dublin's architecture of the great age. In five volumes the Georgian Society did the really essential part of what is being done far more thoroughly but oh so slowly in London by the London Survey Committee. Admitted, of course, that the Dublin work merely skimmed the cream—but what cream!

Before Mahaffy there was a whole hierarchy of Dublin characters of all kinds: Fenian leaders like John O'Leary, orators like Dan O'Connell and Grattan, eccentrics such as "Buck" Whaley with his extravagant bets, leaping out of

108   James Joyce
From the painting by Jacques Emile
Blanche

109   W. B. Yeats
From the painting by J. B. Yeats

110   George Russell (Æ)
From the painting by Sarah Purser

111 Sir John Pentland Mahaffy
From the painting by Sir William Orpen

112   St. Patrick's Cathedral: the memorials to Swift and Stella in the
south aisle of the nave

windows, walking round St. Stephen's Green against time, playing handball by the walls of Jerusalem. Ballad-singers and mendicants, peers and politicians, learned or superficial: Dublin has had enough and to spare. But there is one figure that after a lapse of two hundred years still dominates all the rest; that of Jonathan Swift. Wherever you go in Dublin, whatever books you read, whenever you take part in conversation, Swift will crop up. This has nothing to do with local patriotism or any exaggerated idea of Swift's importance to Dublin. His scale as a thinker and writer overtops ten generations as easily as Michael Collins' as a man of action outdoes one. Interest in Swift's life, and curiosity as to its mysteries is probably more intense now than it has ever been, and shows no sign of abatement. Of course the real mystery about Swift has nothing to do with his origins, or with his relations to Vanessa and Stella, intriguing as these may be to the historian, but how did he come to think in the way he did, with such power and with such expression? In an age given over to acute metaphysics and abstract speculation, Swift went straight to the point; his mind had an edge like a razor, but the weight of a sledge. By straightforward thought and the cool ability to face facts he reached a position where the rest of humanity are unable to follow.

Uncomfortable facts—yes. Long before Whitman thought of going to live with the animals, Swift had been there, and his discoveries led him to chart out a new world for human faith and human courage to conquer. It is commonplace to reject the vision of the Houyhnhnms as the outpourings of a mind diseased, of a great character warped by disappointment, envy, and spiritual pride. But this is not a fair and just estimate: Swift was centuries in advance of his own time, and it is to be feared still centuries ahead of us. We shall not have learnt his lesson until it is possible for every thinking man to say with truth: my kind no longer behave less nobly than the Houyhnhnms. Perhaps we may discern some ray from the future lightening Swift's city Dublin, for there is there a standard of behaviour, mental rather than physical, which does at least reach out, yearns after the human, or rather the horsical.

By way of Swift we come to another of the outstanding facts about Dublin, that the city as we know it is to all intents and purposes a creation of his time and since his time. The over-restored remains of two cathedrals, one chapter-house, a few oddments of parish churches, a section of city wall, a castle tower—nothing else in Dublin will take us back before the Restoration. Later on I shall have a little to say of the doings and institutions of the Middle Ages, on top of which present Dublin is founded. But they are the dim writings of a palimpsest, glimpsed through thoroughpaced erasure and between the sharp and clear-cut letters of a later age. Dublin is not, as are London and Paris, the combined product of several ages, but the child of one. One might think that this would imply living in and on the past, but the literary revival and the political revolution have proved that that is not the case. But the past in Dublin is an enthralling one, and as outsiders we can afford to linger in it. We may ask, for instance, how it was that the age that produced Dublin made such a different city here from the ones it achieved in London or in Bath. What are the factors that make of Dublin a spiritually satisfying place, while work of the same period elsewhere leaves an emotional and aesthetic gap?

Georgian Groupers, who are as pervasive (and dare I add, as soul-shattering) as the Oxford Group, will regard this as heresy. But I can only state plainly that I find the Georgian art of London intensely unsatisfying, and singularly empty of legitimate purpose. The felt want is closely analogous to the moral and social insipidity of the English eighteenth century, and possibly even more of the English social shibboleths which have survived from it into another and more dynamic epoch. For at the best the eighteenth century in Western Europe was a swansong—when the singer was a Mozart, a thing of exquisite beauty. At the worst, it was a clockwork doll running down. Remember that the one truly great man of mid-Georgian London society was the crude provincial, Sam Johnson, and remember the long and uphill fight against polite indifference that his career represents. The time is only redeemed by the scientific curiosity and inventiveness of such men as Daines Barrington and Sir Joseph Banks; the lively wit and fine writing of a Horace Walpole; and the faculty of appreciation which made it possible for Sheridan's plays and Haydn's symphonies to find an audience and to make a profit.

Johnson found that London had everything that life can afford; but he was thinking of the pleasures of learned

113   St. Stephen's Green with the statue of George II
From the aquatint by James Malton

114   St. Stephen's Green

115   The Royal Dublin Society's grounds, Ballsbridge

conversation, the meeting of celebrities, and the opportunities for wit and repartee. Though conscious of his worth, he was not a vain man, and would have been surprised to know that he himself brought to these gatherings the one thing that London could *not* afford, because it had none—a sense of reality. Perhaps Johnson was created a freak to give Boswell his chance; but whatever the cause, his sayings and those of King George III are the only ones in the age that have the full clear ring of sense and humanity. So far as London was concerned, it was an age of pretence. Reality was only injected by the foreigners and the provincials: Handel, Mozart, Haydn, Goldsmith, Sheridan, Johnson, Garrick. And a good deal of the London that the age left behind it is also a thing of pretence; a thin veneer of stereotyped fashion, housing *à la mode*.

There are two main reasons why Georgian architecture and art generally are less vacuous in the provinces than in London: the employment of local craftsmen, and the use of local materials. In the seventeenth century, London itself had employed genuine building craftsmen, many of them provincial, to design as well as build sturdy houses for city merchants and others. There are still a few unbombed houses of that period in the city, and a few in Lincoln's Inn Fields and Wardour Street (the latter hidden behind later fronts). But by the later eighteenth century the amateur architect and the book of the latest designs reigned supreme, and London architecture lost heart. A much better state of affairs reigned at Bath, and still more at Stamford, Exeter, Warwick or York, or for that matter almost any other provincial town with money to spend. London of course has no local building stone, stucco is a poor thing, and unadorned stock brick is unworthy of the higher flights when new, and incomparably dingy with age.

Though I regret the classical pattern-book trimmings which even the provincial architects picked up, I yield to none in admiration of the English vernacular which still produced excellent and lively work up to the time of Victoria. But for the most part it was not great art, but simple and unpretentious, little and good. In other words, it possessed the appropriate provincial virtues, but tells us little or nothing of the main stream. In Dublin it is otherwise. The mere fact that it was a capital city put even the minor craftsmen on their mettle; and major architects from London were inspired by their new surroundings to think and to build better than they knew. The spirit of Dublin infected them, and they unbuttoned; their new patrons, men drawing enormous revenues out of broad Irish acres, could afford to loosen their purse-strings; ground had not the same relative value as in London, and frontages need not be cramped down to an economic but inartistic minimum. Thus planning, design, composition, quality of workmanship, and all the minutiae that go to make up the soul of a building prospered as they had never in the British Isles prospered since the death of the Middle Ages.

Then again, Dublin had and has three admirable local materials: calp limestone from the ground of the city itself, granite from the nearby mountains, and brick of rich red and purple shades of excellent quality and unusual beauty. Furthermore, there stood behind the materials and the crafts- men the compact and unified spirit of a small but capable and witty community: the Dublin wits, the Dublin scientists, and the Dublin craftsmen all had something to impart to one another, in the street, in the Irish Academy, or through the classes and competitions of the Royal Dublin Society. To a great extent this is still true of Dublin, and we must make enlarged allowances for the dynamic age of Sheridan, Grattan and Thomas Ivory.

A page or so back I had some hard things to say about the eighteenth century; and in London especially it was a blind alley with no happy outcome. But let us admit that it was an age that still believed in civilization and in human unity: the mind boggles at the thought of Sterne's *Sentimental Journey* to Paris, in time of war and *without a passport.* Even under Napoleon, Jenner could travel through hostile France, have an audience of the Emperor, and actually secure the release of some British prisoners. There are no two ways about it: in certain directions humanity has dimmed, had the worst of it in the struggle for existence. The ever-open door of the United States has turned into the ever-ready concentra- tion camp of Ellis Island; the English right of asylum and freedom for the escaping slave have become a bitter irony in a country enslaved by proliferating officialdom.

Luckily for Dublin, and for the world, nothing quite like this has happened in Ireland, and men may still be human beings without fear of the consequences. And so the Dublin of the present day is the organic outcome of its dynamic past —it has grown physically and spiritually, by fits and starts, but it has gone on growing. Its being is like that of an onion with its concentric skins, or even more a shallot, surrounded by fresh nuclei of vitality as the old fire dies down. Looking at Dublin's past we shall be peeling off the skins, and finding each one complete, a separate entity, yet fused into the one whole. We are not yet in a position to assess the value of the latest skin, the era of George Moore, Wilde, Yeats (**109**), Synge and James Joyce (**108**), all born within the thirty years from 1853 to 1882. But we can see from the mere list of famous names how great and how constant has been the contribution of Dublin to the mental life of the preceding two centuries.

Without counting Irishmen not specially connected with the capital by birth or education, the succession of distinguished men is striking. Born in the early nineteenth century were the scientists Sir William Rowan Hamilton (1805–65), a universal genius and discoverer of Quaternions, and John Tyndall (1820–93). Literature was represented by the poet James Mangan (1803–49) (**18**), and by the novelists Charles Lever (1806–72) and Joseph Sheridan Le Fanu (1814–73), not to speak of the great historian W. H. Lecky (1838–1903). Art produces the names of the sculptors John Hogan and John Foley (1818–74), and the composer Michael Balfe (1808–70), who with his compatriot William Vincent Wallace (1814–65) made the only Early Victorian music able to stand the test of time.

Going back a further half-century we find Richard Brinsley Sheridan (1751–1816) (**133**) brilliant as wit, dramatist and orator, and a man of noble generosity of heart in a chilly age; Tom Moore (1779–1852), still in spite of unmerited ridicule the national poet; Charles Robert Maturin (1782–1824), pioneer of the "thriller"; the great Duke of Wellington (1769–1852); Sir Martin Archer Shee the painter (1770–1850); and the original musician John Field (1782–1837). These were the harvest of the greatest age of Dublin, but even earlier were the statesmen and orators Edmund Burke (1729–97) and Henry Grattan (1746–1820); Oliver Goldsmith (1728–74) (**7**); and the painter Nathaniel Hone (1718–84), who has never yet received the full recognition that is his due. The seventeenth century saw the birth of the overwhelming Jonathan Swift (1667–1745); of Sir Richard Steele (1672–1729); of Thomas

Parnell the poet (1679–1718); and the eccentric but brilliant philosopher George Berkeley (1685–1753). In a class by himself was Dr. Bartholomew Mosse, founder of the Rotunda (132).

Such is a mere recital of the main strata of Dublin's world-famous names, omitting on the one hand the men such as Sterne, whose Irish mother and birth brought him sensibly within the orbit of Dublin wit; and on the other the vast concourse of names in the front rank of the professions—the great physicians and surgeons, the antiquaries, the natural scientists. But there is a particular class which does deserve more detailed discussion: the architects and building craftsmen who provided housing for the successive generations of Dubliners, and whose hands fashioned the actual fabric of the city as we see and touch it to-day. These men, whether Dubliners, Irish, English, Scots or foreign immigrants, were in a very real sense the makers of Dublin.

As with the thinkers and writers, it is still too early to assess the architects of the most modern developments of the city. There is undoubtedly a school (if I may be allowed for once to use this much abused word) of truly modern designers able, without any concessions to past decorative forms or even to traditional materials, to carry forward the rhythm of the older tradition. Such a work is Mr. Desmond Fitzgerald's Collinstown Airport (117), and another is the pleasing modern house just below the Sandycove Martello Tower, whose massive curves are echoed in a fine terminal bay, semicircular on plan, of glazed metal window; here is what most people would call a modernist dwelling, yet its fine composition and careful siting make it an embellishment to the natural beauty of the tiny harbour and rugged point.

The previous generation, during the death-throes of English governmental influence, faltered in its stride. The hand of the late Sir Aston Webb lay very heavy indeed on the College of Science in Upper Merrion Street, an exhibition of Edwardian pomposity in its most Elgarian mood. At an even more dismal period, 1884, Sir Thomas Manly Deane, in collaboration with his father Sir Thomas Newenham Deane, designed the buildings which house the National Museum and Library (48). These, however, are not crude and heavy, but add to their noble Roman ideas and detail a certain spice of true Dublin manners. I have already mentioned the unusual buildings of Benjamin Woodward, designed under Ruskin's

116   Department of Industry and Commerce, Kildare
Street, 1939–42
J. R. Boyd Barrett, architect

117   Collinstown Airport, 1937–41
Desmond Fitzgerald, architect

MODERN ARCHITECTURE

118 St. Patrick's Cathedral, 1220-60, restored 1863. Interior looking West

influence, which won from Ruskin the description of Woodward as "the only architect in Europe". Even the researches of Mr. C. P. Curran have not thrown a great deal of light on Woodward's origins, though it seems probable that he was born about 1815 in County Cork. He died in middle life in 1861, nine years after entering into partnership with Thomas Deane the first. The Kildare Street Club, Trinity College Engineering School (**119, 120**), and Oxford Museum, Curator's House, and Union Debating Hall were Woodward's chief works. Of them all the only really happy building is the Engineering School (1853–5), whose admirable fenestration and plain wall surfaces form a pleasing contrast to much of the fussy work of the time. Woodward's passing vogue at Oxford owed much to his discovery of two most gifted Irish stone-carvers, James O'Shea and his brother. They were men of pronounced character, insubordinate to a degree, though they did to some extent justify Ruskin's faith in the "genius of the unassisted Workman". But he failed to realize that the reason why the O'Sheas could do well what English workmen could not bring off at all, was that Ireland was still a land of living tradition.

Mercifully, there was not a great deal of building done in central Dublin during the mid-Victorian period, but both the ancient cathedrals were subjected to the horrors of well-meant "restoration", which as usual destroyed the greater part of their original character and beauty. Both buildings were in a very dilapidated state, and urgently needed structural repair, but the work actually done was so extensive as to be even more disastrous than contemporary work at English churches. St. Patrick's (**118**) was the earlier sufferer in 1863–7, but escaped comparatively lightly; G. E. Street at Christ Church (**143, 146**) in 1871–8 practically rebuilt the church, destroying in the process the fourteenth-century choir, of unique interest. The money to pay for these vast and ill-conceived amusements, £160,000 for St. Patrick's and £250,000 for Christ Church, was provided by the two great manufacturers of Dublin's liquid refreshment, Sir Benjamin Lee Guinness, and Mr. Henry Roe the distiller, respectively. It has been noted with some amusement that in the south-western window of the St. Patrick's Lady Chapel there is a monument to Sir Benjamin Guinness's only daughter, of whom it is said that in early youth she laboured for the benefit of the poor and "the relief of their Bodily and Spiritual wants", while in the stained glass immediately above is the text "I was thirsty and ye gave me drink".

There is another monument in St. Patrick's with remarkable wording, the statue in the north nave aisle of the Rt. Hon. George Ogle (1742–1814), whose epitaph states: "Of such a man it may be truly and usefully recorded, that he exhibited a perfect model of that exalted refinement which in the best days of our country characterized the Irish Gentleman." It is also worth quoting from Frederick H. Mares: *Photographs of Dublin*, published in 1867 just as St. Patrick's restoration was completed. "The restoration" Mares tells us, "has been most complete, and the glorious old pile presents, as nearly as possible, the same appearance as it did over 600 years ago. Such portions of new work as it was found necessary to introduce are carefully copied from the original design; in fact, very much of the old structure still remains visible, or has been simply recased, where the stonework had suffered from the effects of either fire or water—the accidents or neglect of centuries. It is now considered the finest and most complete specimen of mediaeval architecture in Ireland".

Unconscious humour also appears in Philip Dixon Hardy's *Tourist's Guide* to Counties Dublin and Wicklow, of the 1850's. Referring to Mountjoy Prison, he remarks that "it has been recently erected, on the plan of Pentonville Prison—its interior is well worthy of notice". The "Rotundo is a fine edifice" and Rutland Square "is laid out in gravel walks and shrubberies, which in the evenings of the summer months are lighted up with lamps, and afford a delightful promenade to the citizens, military bands always attending". This gives us some idea of the delights of Dublin experienced by visitors to the great Dublin Exhibition of 1853, but most of Hardy's descriptions are very commonplace and consist largely of repetitions of the handy adjectives, "fine", "elegant", and "noble". Endless information is provided by the Directories which run from 1773. To take a random example from *The Treble Almanack* for 1832, we are told of the Shelter for Females discharged from Prison, Circular Road, Harcourt Street:

> The Ladies Association for bettering the condition of Female Prisoners in the City and Co. of Dublin, have opened the above Asylum for such wretched Females as, on their removal from prison, have evinced a total change of mind, by earnestly

119 Trinity College Engineering School, 1853-5
Benjamin Woodward, architect

120 Staircase of the Engineering School

121–122 DUBLIN LIFE IN GEORGIAN HOUSES. The doorway on the right is at No. 35 Sean MacDermott (formerly Gloucester) Street

imploring any SHELTER from their formerly depraved state, and willingly submit to *hard fare, strict discipline,* and *continual labour,* until such time as the superintendents may feel justified in recommending them to suitable situations.

We may feel a certain curiosity as to the number of females so wretched as to accept this charitable hard fare, etc., and are not unrewarded by a continued perusal:

Twenty have been sheltered within the year. . . . Six have returned to their friends; one went out to service, and Fourteen were discharged at their own request.

Thirty-eight females at present in the house; the number may be increased to fifty, if means are contributed by the affluent and humane.

N.B.—Washing, Mangling, and Plain Work, taken in and carefully executed.*

The poor and depraved were in the ascendant. Ever since the Union Dublin had been financially depressed, while increasing in population, largely owing to the constant influx from the country, which has ever since continued. The population is now half-a-million; in 1900 it was rather under 300,000; in 1850, 260,000; in 1800, 200,000. About 1750 it stood in the region of 130,000, and a century earlier was perhaps 50,000. It assists comparison to note that in 1801 the London County area contained rather over 800,000 inhabitants, Paris less than 550,000, and Vienna about 230,000. Owing partly to the exodus of English civil servants and sympathizers after 1921, and partly to the steady drift from rural Ireland, the Protestant population of Dublin has decreased relatively in the last fifty years, though in actual numbers it has slightly advanced. The approximate figures for 1891 were 200,000 Roman Catholics out of a total of 245,000; and in 1936, 417,000 Catholics out of 468,000. Protestants still provide a larger share of the learned and professional classes than their total numbers would suggest.

The great problem that arose in the second half of the nineteenth century, and which still persists, is that of tenement houses (**123**). Before 1850 they were a rarity, and confined to a very few poor-class streets; by 1918 they covered the whole

* Charity is also exemplified by the balloon voyage of Mr. Livingston on 27 June, 1822, "on which day he ascended from Portobello Barracks, for the benefit of the suffering poor of the South and South West of Ireland".

of the north city except for a few areas already reconstructed. The figures are dreadful: at the census of 1911 the population of the whole north city was over 160,000, and of these more than one-quarter, 41,000 persons comprising 12,000 families, were living in little over 3,000 tenement houses—of these only 627 were classed as "first-class" houses, and housed nearly

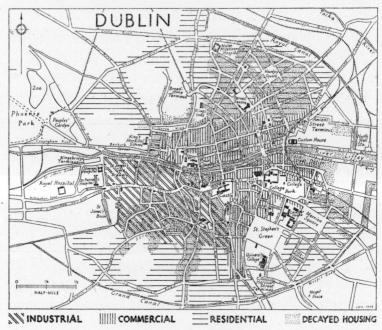

123 Dublin demography

3,800 families consisting of 12,500 people. Over 5,500 families, of nearly 16,000 persons, occupied one-room tenements at rents varying from 6d. to 5s. 6d. a week. Certain streets, among them the most aristocratic of the northern quarters, descended to the abyss at a fearful rate. Dominick Street, which had one tenement house in 1850, had 75 (out of a total of 145 houses) in 1918; Gloucester Street with 5 in 1850 had 81; Marlborough Street, 2 in 1850, 50 (out of 116) in 1918 (**124**).

The case of Lower Dominick Street provides one of the most poignant contrasts. In 1785 it contained the residences of two peers, six members of the Irish Commons, a judge of the King's Bench and half-a-dozen other barristers, three sheriffs peers, the Seneschal of the King's Manors, the City Chaplain, and several attornies, doctors and other professional men. By 1800, the year of the Union, the legal element was increasing; lawyers occupied 26 houses in 1834 and 31 in 1850, but by that time there were 10 houses vacant. In 1875 the legal element had sunk to 17, there were nine "merchants", two hotels and a boarding-house, three schools, a marble-yard,

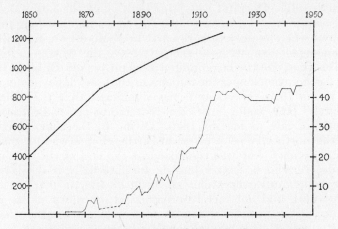

124 Tenement houses in Dublin: thick line shows totals,
1850–1918; thin line, Lower Dominick Street, 1863–1946

two coachbuilders, a builder, a printer, a surveyor, an architect and a tobacconist. In 1900 only two lawyers were left, and there were 11 tenement houses; by 1925 there were 41 tenements, and by 1946, 44, while private houses had sunk to two, and two adjacent houses were occupied as the Duke of Leinster's estate office, where formerly had been his town-house. Valuations, which in 1850 were about £60, and ran as high as £110, have now dropped, in spite of the fall in the value of money, to a level of about £25, and varying from £50 down to £7 10s.

Dublin was hard hit by the Union, which took away at one fell swoop Parliament, nobility, commons men, and all the many hangers-on of state who spent their money in the city. The seventeen years of high summer were over, and it was not merely to its former state of dependence that Dublin was reduced, but to the status of a mere provincial town. Add to this the general depression caused by Revolutionary and Napoleonic Wars, and the wonder is not that dire poverty should have come, but that its advent was so long postponed. For the inner city was still in process of building for a quarter-century after the Union: Mountjoy Square (**158**) was not finished until 1818, and Fitzwilliam Square not until 1825. Even later than this the plans were showing the projected Royal Circus at the top of Eccles Street, where the Mater Misericordiae Hospital was later built—but the hospital did not acquire its plot until 1853. The circus had not long been set out when its projector, the first Lord Mountjoy, was killed in an engagement with the rebels of 1798; the '98 was in more senses than one the beginning of the end for old Dublin. But for a generation longer the remains of the ascendancy managed to retain their power, and it is significant that the "Black Church" (**159**) could have been required as a new Protestant chapel-of-ease as late as 1830. Owing to the sharp decline of the north city soon afterwards, the chapel was for many years derelict, but was re-opened at the end of the century. It deserves to be better known, for internally it displays a parabolic vault generations ahead of its time, a mark of the structural, and not merely ornamental ingenuity of its designer, John Semple, who also was architect for the quasi-Portuguese Gothic church at Monkstown, and for a great deal of spike-Gothic rebuilding of out-county churches under the Board of First Fruits.

The development of planning took place in several distinct waves: the first of importance was in the reign of Charles II, during Ormonde's viceroyalty (**125**). This was the period of the first expansion on the north side of the Liffey, and included the building of four new bridges and the laying out of Capel Street. On the south side, under the auspices of the corporation, a great change had begun a little earlier, in the enclosure and allotment of the common land which was to become St. Stephen's Green and its surrounding houses, starting in 1663. So far as this period can be referred to an architect, it is the work of Sir William Robinson, Surveyor-General of Works and Fortifications in Ireland, and architect of the Royal Hospital, Kilmainham. After a pause, broken only by the building of Thomas Burgh's great Library (**10, 11**) at Trinity

College (1712–32), Pearce's new Parliament House (1728–39), and the making of the quays (*c.* 1717–20), a new period of development was reached, which may be called the age of Richard Cassels, its main architect. Cassels, a German brought to Ireland about 1727 by Sir Gustavus Hume, is known to have been born at Cassel in Hesse, and Mr. Curran has shown

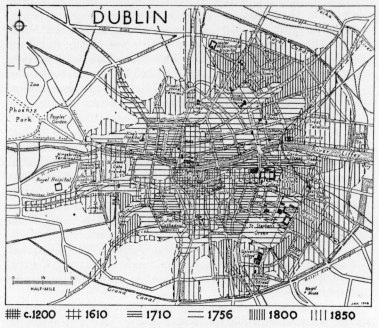

125 The growth of Dublin

that his surprisingly austere version of Palladian architecture derives from the work of French Huguenot refugees, who after a period of work in Holland, settled in Cassel as architects and town-planners under the Landgrave of Hesse. Mr. Curran thinks that members of the family may already have been settled in Ireland before Richard Cassels' arrival. He died in 1751, so that the period of his work in Ireland was less than twenty-five years.

North of the river, Cassels designed Tyrone House (1740) and the Rotunda Hospital (1750), which was mainly carried

89

out by his pupil John Ensor (130). At an earlier date, c. 1730, he had built some large private houses in Henrietta Street, which had been first set out in 1721. On the south side he designed several houses in St. Stephen's Green, most notable among them being No. 85 (1739), better known as Clanwilliam House; the Dining Hall and Printing-house (1734) of Trinity College; and above all, Leinster House (1745–8). Leinster House was doubly significant: as the largest and most magnificent of Dublin mansions, built for the premier peer of Ireland, the Earl of Kildare and from 1766 Duke of Leinster, it set a fashion in noble and costly building; secondly, the Earl having determined to lead the world of fashion away from the north to the south bank, the building of his seat resulted in the development of the south-eastern quarter to a position of pre-eminence which it still occupies (131). Between Grafton Street, the St. Stephen's Green Land, and Patrick's Well Lane (now Nassau Street) lay Mynchen's Fields, once the property of the nunnery of St. Mary de Hogge. The western half of this land was leased by the first Viscount Palmerston to Joshua Dawson in 1705; Dawson two years later laid out the street which bears his name, and in 1710 built at the south-eastern corner of the property the house which he sold to the City for £3,500 in 1715, to become the Mansion House, official residence of the Lord Mayor.

The eastern half of Mynchen's Fields belonged to the first Viscount Molesworth, who left it by will to his sons in 1725. As he set a limit of 81 years to any building leases, no one would take up plots until the second Viscount obtained an Act to extend the leases to 99 years: about 1727 Molesworth Street and Coote Street (later Kildare Street) were laid out, but the whole of the land East of Coote Street was bought by the Earl of Kildare in 1744. As this strip of ground was not spacious enough, the earl leased ground on the eastern side from the fields of his neighbour, Viscount Fitzwilliam of Merrion. This leased ground formed the site of the famous Leinster Lawn. For some years development was halted on the south side, until Viscount Fitzwilliam decided to lay out the citywards portion of his vast estates; but this stage of growth is a later story (135, 136).

At Cassels' death, Upper Sackville Street and Rutland Square had been laid down as a result of compromise between the ideas of Luke Gardiner, owner of the bulk of the land, and

Dr. Bartholomew Mosse (**132**), founder of the Lying-In Hospital, afterwards to be famous as the Rotunda, from its circular assembly room. Mosse's brilliant and original idea

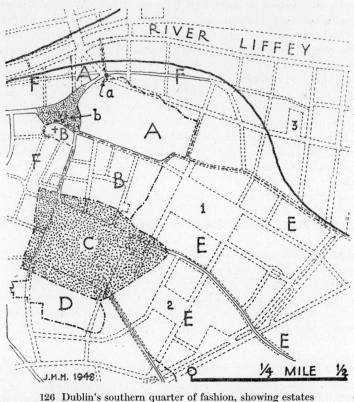

126 Dublin's southern quarter of fashion, showing estates

A College Land
B Minchin Fields
C St. Stephen's Green
D Lord Clonmel's House and Lawn
E Fitzwilliam Estate

F Corporation Land
a The Long Stone
b The Thing Mount
1 Merrion Square
2 Fitzwilliam Square
3 Queen's Square

Shaded areas are old commons. Firm lines mark ancient roads.

was that the profits of assembly rooms and gardens should support the hospital, and as long as there was a fashionable world in the north city to patronize his scheme, it prospered. By 1756 the east side of Rutland Square was built, by ten years later the west side, while the northern end was filled between 1762 and 1769. Cassels' pupil and partner, John Ensor, had a large share in the work, but for the most important mansion in the square, Charlemont House (12) on the north, designs were sent from England by Sir William Chambers, who shortly afterwards provided the Earl of Charlemont with the drawings for the famous little Casino at Marino, built at a cost of £60,000 between 1765 and 1771 (105). Chambers also designed the Trinity College Chapel and Examination Hall (1781), both carried out by Graham Myers, for Chambers was never in Ireland. He is often credited with the main front to College Green, but this was built in 1752–60 by Henry Keene and John Sanderson of London.

If we count the period of Robinson as the first wave of Dublin's expansion, and the age of Cassels as the second, the third was ushered in by the appointment of the Wide Streets Commissioners in 1757. They straightway laid out Parliament Street (59) and for two generations busied themselves in sensible and sensitive town-planning and improvement of the best kind. Meanwhile, Lord Fitzwilliam's schemes began to burgeon, and John Ensor, who had had the experience of building a large part of Rutland Square, was called across the river to lay out the square which was to take its owner's title of Merrion (135). The first scheme was laid down in 1762, and two years later building began. At this time it was intended to carry the square on to a new street a good deal farther East than the present Fitzwilliam Street, but the present dimensions had been adopted by 1780, and this settled the lines of the next stage of progress.

The next was in fact the final stage; it was the direct outcome of the prosperity induced by the independent Irish Parliament of 1783. There was during the next few years an absolute orgy of building, much of it on a grand scale. At the end of the preceding period had come Thomas Cooley's Royal Exchange (1769–79) and Thomas Ivory's Blue-Coat School (1773–83); and Cooley's scheme had been prepared for the new Four Courts (53). John Beresford, Chief Commissioner of the Irish Revenue, had in 1781 persuaded James Gandon to leave England for Dublin, to become architect for the great new Customs House which Beresford projected (50). Gandon, a dynamic, forceful personality, settled in Dublin permanently, and was soon called in to take charge

128 Powerscourt House, William Street,
1774–8
James McCullagh, plasterer

127 The Casino, Marino: interior
Sir William Chambers, architect

129   The Rutland Fountain, Merrion Square, 1791.   Henry A. Baker, architect

From an aquatint by J. G. Stadler

of the spate of new works. Born in 1743, he had been apprenticed to Sir William Chambers, and in 1769 won the first gold medal for architecture awarded by the Royal Academy. He built not only the Custom House (1781–91) but the East Portico of the Parliament House (1785), the Four Courts (1786–96), and the King's Inns (1795–1817), the last in collaboration with his pupil Henry A. Baker, and completed by Francis Johnston. Baker was also the designer of the Rutland Fountain (1791) at the west end of Merrion Square, opposite the Leinster Lawn (**129**).

The second phase of Dublin's last age of architecture was Francis Johnston's; his brother Richard Johnston had designed the New Rooms (**22**) (now the Gate Theatre) at the Rotunda (1784–6) with advice from Gandon, and in the work done for the new Union administration, Francis takes the premier place. He seems to have been everywhere and done almost everything, and it is not surprising that some of his work should be unsatisfactory. I have enumerated his more important Dublin buildings, but he also worked on a large scale elsewhere in Ireland. Mr. John Betjeman and Mr. Colm O'Lochlainn have dealt with Johnston in great detail, and I must refer the reader to their papers for a full account. Besides the buildings I have already noted, he designed in the outskirts of Dublin, the Foundling Hospital, now the South Dublin Union (1798–1804), the Richmond Bridewell, later Wellington Barracks (1811–17), and the Royal Hibernian School in the Phoenix Park (1808–13). His most generally famous building (apart from the Post Office) is St. George's Church (1802–13), a sort of modified St. Martin-in-the-Fields, but lacking the vigour and sound construction of Gibbs's masterpiece (**40**). Johnston gave the roof of St. George's the enormous span of 65 feet, but failing to devise a proper construction, it nearly collapsed in 1836, and was only saved by the insertion of iron arches by two Dublin engineers, John and Robert Mallet.

While architecture was proceeding step by step, Dublin was growing up in other ways. Public street-lighting had been introduced in 1697, superseding the earlier system described by Mr. Patrick Meehan, of setting forth a lantern and candle-light at every fifth house during the winter months. The Grand Canal was begun in 1765, and reached Sallins in 1782; it was at Monasterevan in 1786 and Athy in 1791. The capital of the company was £200,000, and it might have been a great financial success, but for the forming of a rival company, the Royal Canal, which instead of striking out into unopened country, followed an almost parallel route, to the mutual destruction of both parties. Mail coaches did not begin to run until 1790, and so only had a life of some fifty years until they were seriously rivalled by the railways. In 1832, the heyday of the stage coaches, there was to most large towns in Ireland a Night Coach and also a Day Coach, the Night vehicle carrying the mail. On the routes traversed by the canals there were elaborately fitted passenger boats, and the richly appointed hotels noticed before. By 1832 navigation was by steamboat, leaving Dublin twice every day. In 1773 a penny-post had been instituted within the city and suburbs as far out as four miles. For many years this had quite separate receiving offices and staff from those which dealt with the Mail proper. The general advance in material civilization was particularly reflected by the founding of the Dublin Society in 1731, and its incorporation in 1750. Its original purpose was "for improving Husbandry, Manufactures, and other Useful Arts", and the word "Sciences" was almost immediately added to its title. Under the Irish Parliament, the Society received a large grant in aid of its researches and its system of prizes and premiums, but this support was soon reduced after the Union. Among the most important efforts of the Society were its classes in art, and it formed a splendid library, which was handed over to government to become the nucleus of the National Library in 1877.

Of course even societies can only do a limited amount of good, but the Dublin Society has always been, and still is, exceptional. Every one of the thousands of visitors to the August Horse Show is in a position to realize that (115). The whole of the preparations for this colossal spectacle, and the prestige which carries it off with clockwork success, are the result entirely of enlightened private enterprise. This has always been a noteworthy characteristic of Dubliners: one of the most amazing examples of private enterprise ever known was the publication by Edward Viscount Kingsborough, son of the third earl of Kingston, of the *Antiquities of Mexico*, at a cost to himself of over £32,000. The work, consisting of facsimiles of all the native manuscripts that survived the Spanish Conquest of Mexico, appeared in seven volumes,

130   The Rotunda Hospital, 1750-7; before additions
Richard Cassels, architect

131   Leinster House, now An t-Oireachtas, 1745–8
Richard Cassels, architect

133   Richard Brinsley Sheridan
From a pastel by John Russell, 1788

132   Dr. Bartholomew Mosse
From the bust at the Rotunda, 1757

imperial folio, at a price of £210, and a further two volumes were issued posthumously at £254. Kingsborough, who lived at No. 3 Henrietta Street, bankrupted himself, was arrested for debt by a paper manufacturer, and died of typhus in the Dublin Debtors' Prison at the age of 40. Prescott wrote, very truly, that "by this munificent undertaking, which no government probably would have, and few individuals could have executed, he has entitled himself to the lasting gratitude of every friend of science".

Among the classes promoted by the Dublin Society were courses in arts and crafts, and these had considerable influence on the ornament used by, for example, the very important body of Dublin plasterworkers. This important subject has been dealt with in minute detail by Mr. C. P. Curran, who has traced out the several phases of stucco design, and also the careers of most of the men responsible. So far as the Dublin Society's schools are concerned, they were set up in 1742, being the first to give general public instruction in the arts, apart from the French Academy of Painting. The Dublin schools, on the other hand, seem to have been the first in the world to have been open to both sexes. There were three separate schools, teaching Ornament, Figure, and Drawing in Architecture: in 1766 the number of new students was 111, while in 1810 the School of Ornament alone took in 505, and over 300 were at work on the Figure. The first teacher of ornament (from 1746) was a Frenchman, James Mannin, who was still at work in 1766. The results of academic work in architecture have generally been unfortunate, apart from the cases of exceptional men like Gandon, but in eighteenth-century Dublin there was unusual scope for proper instruction unconnected with the craft guilds, which were open only to Protestants.

Mr. Curran divides Dublin plasterwork into four main periods: (1) the compartment ceiling and the late Louis XIV style, definitely pre-rococo, and in vogue before 1740; (2) from about 1740 to 1755 a period of developing rococo, with the figured ceiling brought to Ireland by the Italian brothers Paul and Philip Francini in 1739; (3) the richly naturalistic ornament, with birds and floral motives, particularly typical of Dublin, and dating from 1755 to 1770; (4) finally, the academic style introduced by Robert Adam, but carried out by native craftsmen. In 1759–60 three out of the six Dublin banks failed, and this economic check corresponds with a gap in the main stream of building work. Of early Dublin plaster-work the only important example is the chapel ceiling at the Royal Hospital, Kilmainham (1686); in the first period of "magnificence" when Henrietta Street was built, Edward Simpson seems to have been the chief plasterer at work; then came the influence of the Francini, who had been engaged at No. 15 Queen's Square, Bath, in 1729, were working at Carton, Co. Kildare from 1739, and who left Dublin by about 1756; later, the great exponent of birds in high relief (16 inches from the surface at No. 20 Dominick Street) was Robert West, master builder and plasterer, freeman in 1752, who died in 1790 (**140**).

The work in Clanwilliam House (No. 85 St. Stephen's Green) is by the Francini; that next door, at No. 86, comprising in all 63 birds, is by Robert West, who was also the builder and decorator of No. 20 Dominick Street, shortly before 1755. Plaster birds had first appeared in Dublin in 1730, and the high-water mark of the craft was reached in 1751 at Mespil House, near Upper Leeson Street, where magnificent panels of the elements and seasons show strong French influence (**139**). The artist of Mespil House is unknown, but one French stuccodore is known to have been employed in Dublin, Bartholomew Cramillion, who produced the unique baroque work in the chapel of the Rotunda Hospital, carried out in 1756, five years after Cassels' death (**134, 141**). In the final academic period, the leading man was Michael Stapleton, a master builder like Robert West (whose executor he was), Thomas Ivory and the Ensors. Among his known work as a plasterer are the principal rooms of Powerscourt House (1771-8), the Examination Hall of Trinity College (1777), and the splendid series of ceilings at Belvedere House (*c.* 1775). He also did work for the Chief Secretary's Lodge in 1784, and for Vice-regal Lodge in 1787. Stapleton died in 1801, but his son George carried out stucco tracery and ornaments in the Castle Chapel for Francis Johnston (1807–14). Other import-ant men of this period were James McCullagh, who flourished from 1751 to 1786, and executed the plasterwork of the hall and staircase at Powerscourt House (**128**); and Charles Thorp the elder, freeman in 1772, Lord Mayor 1800–01, and died *c.* 1817, who made the board-room ceiling at the Blue-Coat School in 1778–80, and the ceiling of the Council Chamber, now destroyed, at the City Hall.

134   The Chapel of the Rotunda Hospital: Altar-Piece and Allegory
of Charity, 1757–8
Bartholomew Cramillion, stucco-worker

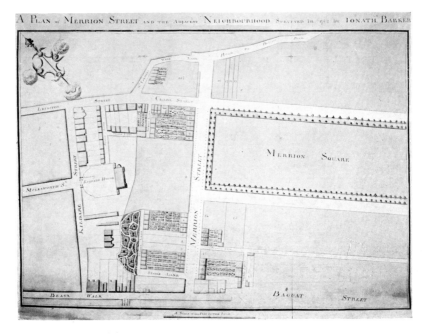

135   Plan of Merrion Square as first set out, 1762
From the original by Jonathan Barker, by permission of the Lord Herbert

M.ʳ Crosbie's Ascent from Leinster Lawn

136   The first Balloon Ascent from Leinster Lawn, 1785

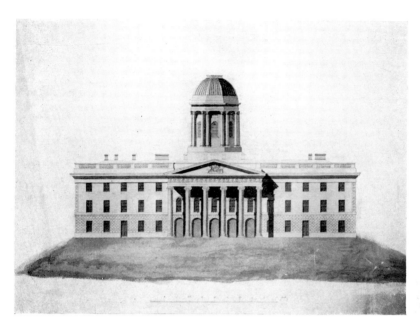

137   Francis Johnston's cupola design for the General Post Office, 1814

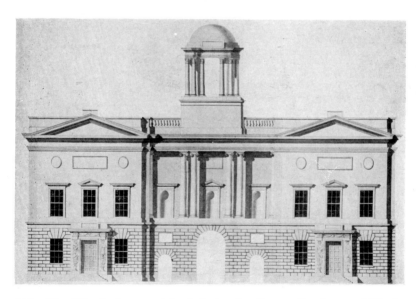

138   The King's Inns: original design by James Gandon and H. A. Baker, 1805

139   Mespil House: detail of ceiling, 1751

In spite of the narrower limitations of this last silver age, a number of very fine mansions were produced, notably Aldborough House (1793–6) on the North Circular Road, said to be from designs by Chambers, and now a Post Office department (**13**); and Clonmel House, Harcourt Street (1776–84), formerly the temporary home of Sir Hugh Lane's art collection, now in the Municipal Gallery at Charlemont House.

Before we say good-bye to Georgian Dublin there are two or three other buildings worth a glance. On Usher's Island stands the melancholy ghost of Moira House, begun in 1752 and in its prime one of the most extravagantly appointed of all the great mansions. Its internal decorations are said to have been by a native artist named Healy, but all are gone now. In 1775 John Wesley waited on Lady Moira, and was surprised to find "a far more elegant room than any I ever saw in England". Its walls were inlaid from floor to ceiling with mother-of-pearl. In 1826 the house was sold to the Mendicity Institution, its top storey was removed, the decorations gutted, and where the cream of eighteenth-century fashion once held sprightly converse, lack-lustre windows now gaze blindly out upon the Liffey, and beggars shuffle to receive their dole. Babylon is fallen indeed. Another building, actually erected as a charitable institution but now a jam factory, is the noble granite-fronted Simpson's Hospital facing the top of Jervis Street. It is on the site of an old brick mansion known as Putland House, which was pulled down in 1787 to make room for the new building. The hospital was completed in 1791 at a cost of just under £6,500. Although built with a very different end in view, it has the same type of rigorously controlled academic front as No. 86 St. Stephen's Green.

Last of all, let us go back to the south side, cross St. Stephen's Green, and pass through Hume Street, now government offices, into Ely place (**43**). Here is the splendid Ely House of 1770, and other smaller houses put up in the succeeding decade. This select backwater was one of the most exclusive haunts of the fashionable world, and notwithstanding the invasion of institutions and government departments, is still one of the few streets in Dublin that retain something of the polish of their illustrious past. It has always been connected with the great legal luminaries of Dublin, and in the past has housed John Philpot Curran, Charles Kendal Bushe,

DUBLIN

and John Fitzgibbon, the envied and hated Earl of Clare. Attorney-General and Lord Chancellor of Ireland, Clare was a man with the most complete disregard of public opinion, and an iron courage which he certainly required. In 1795 his house (No. 6) was attacked by an immense mob, and would have been burst open but for Clare's foresight. At the end of his garden, over a back wall, were the premises of Thomas Brown, a master builder of Lower Baggot Street, and knowing that an attack was probable, Clare had arranged with Brown to barricade the house in secret, smuggling the materials across the garden.

It is difficult to picture a furious and undisciplined mob in the reserved calm of Ely Place, but one can recapture something of the spirit of a more recent but no less historic phase of its existence. At No. 4 in the southern arm of the Place, George Moore lived during his strange and prolific return to Ireland. Opposite his house is a queer little garden in which he held dinner parties on summer evenings. For ten years the spirit of the eighteenth century was brought back, and more than that; for while the men of 1790 realized that they were poised on the edge of the abyss, Moore and his friends believed themselves the prophets of a new world. Possibly, human nature being what it is, their expectations were too sanguine, and yet their dreams of a new Ireland have been at least partially realized, and who knows what the future may have in store? The railings of Moore's little garden are rusty, the fruit-trees overgrown, the lawns dug and planted with cabbage, carrot and potato. In the mid-day sun you may see a cat asleep among the rows of onions, or a gardener in his shirt-sleeves enjoying an after-dinner pipe. But come back at sunset and you will catch a glimpse of the enduring Dublin, the city of Swift and Grattan, of poets, patriots, prophets and eccentrics—to all of them, brilliant citizens of no mean city, hail and farewell.

140   No. 20 Lower Dominick Street, *c.* 1755
Robert West, builder and plasterer

141   Rotunda Hospital Chapel: part of ceiling, 1755–7
Bartholomew Cramillion, stucco-worker

142   St. Patrick's Cathedral and Park

143   Christ Church Cathedral from Winetavern Street

Epilogue—Early Dublin

As far as possible I have dealt with Dublin as a single unit, built up of historical layers and topographical sections, but essentially to be understood as one whole. For this reason I have said very little about the story of the English colony on the Liffey before the arrival of its classic age. All the same, this earlier background is of interest, if only because of its analogies to the colonization and development of North America. Bearing in mind the small populations of the Middle Ages, and the difficulties of transport, the settlement of Dublin begins to look a great deal like that of New York.

To the Norman knights of Strongbow's invading force, Ireland was a new world peopled by savages, and Viking Dublin was a ready-made bridge-head as convenient for their purposes in 1170 as Dutch New Amsterdam was to the Duke of York's commanders in 1664. Both cities were trading depots with a large area of backlands from which valuable products could be derived, but controlled by hostile natives. The later history of the two settlements is also closely parallel in some ways; in both cases the English colonists absorbed their predecessors, the Danish Ostmen of Dublin, and the Dutch of New Amsterdam; in both cases they found themselves at loggerheads with their home government; in both cases they received important accessions of strength from foreign refugees who sought religious or political freedom.

No such comparison must be carried too far, and there are glaring differences between the position and development of the two places. But at least Dublin has outdistanced Bristol in importance, if not to the extent that New York now tends to dominate both Amsterdam and London, its progenitors. And the problem of a large pauper population dwelling in tenements has been as grave in the American city as it is in Dublin. New Amsterdam was not founded until 1626, and in just over a hundred years its population was between 8,000 and 9,000. This was almost exactly the same as the number of Dublin's inhabitants in 1644; but whereas the mid-seventeenth century saw Dublin's sudden rise to nearly 70,000 souls in 1682, New York did not reach this point until after 1800, when Dublin had a population of about 190,000. Only by about 1830 did New York outstrip Dublin's population of some 200,000, and then came the great American influx, so that by the time Dublin had reached 300,000 in 1910, New York had 16 times that number.

The seventeenth century in Dublin saw the struggle, decisive for the next two hundred years, between the Catholic and Protestant forces for the control of Ireland. In 1644, just before the Cromwellian occupation, two-thirds of the city population were Protestants, and of course the brutal repression of papistry by Cromwell greatly increased this disproportion for a time. The character of this Protestant "garrison" was made even more Puritan and extremist than it might otherwise have been by the foundation in 1591 of the ultra-puritan Trinity College as a forcing-ground for proselytes. The policy of relative toleration for Catholics introduced by Charles I ended after the temporary Catholic triumph of the Confederation of Kilkenny in 1641. But the beginnings of a more liberal culture had been present during the great Strafford's viceroyalty, when James Shirley the poet had been one of his household, and the first Dublin theatre was opened in Werburgh Street in 1635. After the Puritan set-back, a new theatre was built in Orange Street, later Smock Alley, in 1661. Strafford showed his excellent taste by removing the atrocious Boyle monument, which had usurped the place of the High Altar in St. Patrick's Cathedral. He had also introduced a new style in architecture in the enormous palace he built at Jigginstown, Co. Kildare, between 1633 and 1639. Intended as a vice-regal residence and for the entertainment of Charles I when he should visit Ireland, it had a central block of over 300 feet frontage, with projecting wings at each end increasing the total length to some 380 feet.

Besides the founding of Trinity College, the Elizabethan period had seen a number of improvements in material civilization, in directions where Ireland had lagged far behind England owing to her disturbed state at the close of the Middle Ages. The first public clocks were put up by Queen Elizabeth's orders in 1560, on the Castle, at the Tholsel, and St. Patrick's Cathedral. The head of the city water-supply had been enclosed in 1555—pipes were not laid throughout the city

144　Carlisle Bridge and Lower Sackville Street, *c.* 1875.　The bridge
was built in 1794: James Gandon, architect; and replaced by O'Connell
Bridge in 1880

145　The Wellington Bridge, built in 1816, commonly known as the
Metal or Halfpenny Bridge

147 St. Patrick's Cathedral: north nave aisle

146 Christ Church Cathedral: Lady Chapel from south aisle, 1871–8

George Edmund Street, architect

until 1670. In 1579 the state records were arranged in the Bermingham Tower of the Castle and put in charge of a salaried keeper; and in 1571 printing in Irish characters was first introduced by Nicholas Walsh, chancellor of St. Patrick's. But perhaps the most significant of all the events of the time was the introduction of the potato, certainly grown by Sir Walter Raleigh on his estate at Youghal in 1585. This is about as early as they were grown anywhere in Europe outside Spain, where they had appeared at Seville by 1570. It is often claimed that John Hawkins introduced to England and Ireland in 1565 potatoes from Santa Fé in New Spain, but modern research has shown that these were not true potatoes, but the convolvulus tubers now known as sweet potatoes. Dr. Redcliffe Salaman's fascinating researches into the history of the potato have shown just how it was that Ireland came to suffer to an inordinate degree from the Potato Blight of 1845–6. The potato is a reasonably satisfactory *sole* diet, and can equally be fed to domestic animals: therein lay the danger of its introduction. Its culture demands the minimum of work and attention, and thus exercises a fatal attraction for a people ground down to an absolute minimum standard of living. Further, while the communal open-field system of England and a large part of Europe made the extensive cultivation of potatoes by individuals impossible (for the fields as a whole had to be laid open for pasture after corn harvest), Ireland with its little plots tilled in severalty could and did raise the potato— and nothing else. Raleigh, who notwithstanding his courtly virtues was one of the most rapacious adventurers that ever lived (a portrait of him in the Dublin Portrait Gallery well displays this side of his character) must also take ultimate responsibility for the disaster which caused at least a million deaths from famine and disease, and reduced the population of Ireland from nearly nine million to little over four.

The Middle Ages had had their own allowance of disasters: famine, plague, fire and flood. Dublin experienced the three Black Deaths of the mid-fourteenth century, and a fourth, in 1383, of her own, besides four great plagues in the fifteenth century and one in 1525. There were terrible fires in the city in 1190 and 1282; in 1304 St. Mary's Abbey was largely destroyed, with many of the rolls of the chancery taken there for safe keeping, and in 1362 part of the nave of St. Patrick's Cathedral was burnt, "by negligence of John the Sexton". In 1266 there was a great earthquake; in 1316 Christ Church steeple was blown down; in 1452 the bed of the Liffey in Dublin was mysteriously dry for a distance of two miles. From the 2nd of December 1338 to the following 10th of February the river was frozen over, as it was just over four centuries later, from 29th December 1739 to the 8th February 1740. But of all the calamities that befell, the one longest remembered was "Black Monday", the Easter Monday of 1209, when the Bristol colonists, making holiday in the fields and groves of Cullenswood near Ranelagh, were most unsportingly set upon by the tribesmen from the mountains, and suffered appalling losses; so much so that they had to send to Bristol for reinforcements.

The colonial character of Dublin was long maintained; in lists of the citizens from the late twelfth to the fourteenth centuries, English names vastly predominate. The Dublin "Roll of Names" made within the generation following the conquest includes William the goldsmith of Shrewsbury, Godard the goldsmith of London, and Elias the carpenter of "Barewec" (? Berwick). Between 1225 and 1250 craftsmen admitted to the freedom included Hugh the painter of Derby, Geoffrey and Roger, painters of London, Hugh painter of York, and Henry painter of Kilkenny; Ralph the carver (*talliator*) of Hereford and Nicholas the mason (*cementarius*) of Coventry. In the 1330's John of Corfe, presumably an importation from the Purbeck quarries, was "chief keeper, purveyor and ordainer of all the King's works in Ireland pertaining to the office of masonry" at fees of £6 13s. 4d. a year, and from 1343 to 1359 or later Adam Carleton was chief carpenter of castles and manors and all other the King's works in Ireland, at £9 2s. 6d. John More, mason, and "clerk of the works in Dublin Castle and elsewhere in Leinster" appears in 1372 and again, as we have seen, getting ready to rebuild the Bridge in 1386. More may possibly have been the master who designed Archbishop Minot's grand tower at St. Patrick's about 1363 (**142**). The remains of mouldings and tracery suggest that the work was unusually up-to-date, and thus that the architect was a fairly recent importation from England.

There is practically nothing left suggestive of native Irish work in the two cathedrals or the Dublin parish churches. Before the arrival of the Anglo-Normans, an anglicized form of

148 St. Patrick's Cathedral: Lady Chapel, *c.* 1230–70

149 St. Mary's Abbey: Chapter House, *c.* 1180–90

150   Nave, *c.* 1215   151   Choir, *c.* 1185

Christ Church Cathedral: Carvings

152   Christ Church Cathedral   153   St. Audoen's Church: Font
Triforium in Transept, *c.* 1185

the earliest Gothic had been brought to Ireland by the Cistercians, who founded their first Irish house at Mellifont near Drogheda in 1142, and rapidly spread southwards, to Baltinglass (*c.* 1148) and Jerpoint (1155–8), one of the best preserved of their abbeys. In these early works there are, however, some unusual features traceable to Irish influences and craftsmen. But the colonists of Dublin a generation later brought their own designers and workmen with them, and so we get at Christ Church, begun in 1172, a transplanted cathedral that might have been built in Somerset, so closely does it adhere to the style of Wells and Glastonbury (**143**). The present choir is an imaginary restoration of the original by Street, but the crypt, crossing and transepts are genuine remains of the first work, while the nave was begun in 1213, and its most western bay, differing in detail, in or soon after 1234. The tower, blown down in 1316, was rebuilt in 1330, and the choir removed by Street in 1871 had been built soon after 1350. Not only was the original design English, as well as the colonists who carried it out, but even the carved work itself was of imported English oolite stone.

The other cathedral, St. Patrick's, needs a word of explanation. Why, it may well be asked, two cathedrals in the same place? The answer lies in the conflicting jurisdictions of which I have spoken before. As happened in England in the joint dioceses of Bath and Wells, and Coventry and Lichfield, and as almost happened in the fifteenth century with the see of Worcester, when its bishop wished to erect the collegiate church of Westbury near Bristol into a second cathedral, the archbishop found his position intolerable in a church controlled by a prior and monastic chapter. Christ Church, Dublin, was of course such a monastic house, and John Comyn, the first of the Anglo-Norman archbishops, determined on building a new secular church outside the walls of the city, on land under his own jurisdiction, where he could be fully master. He rebuilt a very ancient church of St. Patrick, and it is possible that the westernmost bay of the south nave aisle of the present cathedral is a survival from this work of 1191–2. But the beginning of the church as it now stands can be dated to 1225, and the Lady Chapel, modelled upon that of Salisbury, was probably finished in the next ten years (**148**). The rest of the work followed through the thirteenth century, and the north-western tower and part of the

nave were rebuilt after 1362, as previously mentioned. The
spire was added in 1749 by the architect and writer on
hydraulic engineering, George Semple.

Closely connected with St. Patrick's was the project of an
Irish University. Pope Clement V granted a Bull in 1312
for the purpose of such a foundation, but no action seems to
have been taken until 1320, when rules were laid down to
govern the masters and scholars of the University. There
were certainly students in 1358, when they were granted a
protection by Edward III, but five years later a petition to
Pope Urban V alleged that there was no Irish *studium*.
However, in 1364 Lionel Duke of Clarence gave land to endow
a lecturer in theology, who was to be an Austin friar, and as
late as 1496 the provincial Synod decreed contributions for
seven years to provide stipends for the university lecturers.
Although, mainly on account of civil disturbances in the later
Middle Ages, the university was not a flourishing concern,
it continued to exist until the dissolution of the cathedral
establishment by Henry VIII. There were attempts to revive
it in 1547, 1565 and 1584, and the new Trinity College of 1591
must be regarded as in some sense a continuation of the
earlier foundation.

By the time of Richard II's visit to Dublin in 1394, the
English position in Ireland had greatly deteriorated; many of
the colonists had intermarried with the natives and adopted
their language; large parts of the country, never entirely
subdued, had been lost outright. Richard's expedition, with
its mingling of pomp, strength, and clemency, was designed
to restore Ireland to the English Crown, and had he been per-
mitted to carry out his second mission, five years later, the
whole course of Anglo-Irish relations would almost certainly
have been changed for the better. But Henry IV and his
successors were not interested in conciliation or even in
Ireland at all, and English influence shrank into a small
area round Dublin known as the Pale. In 1401 the Courts,
which previously had moved about English Leinster, were
transferred from Carlow to Dublin for the last time. The
colony had fallen on evil days, and was perpetually on the
defensive, fighting a losing battle. By 1488 the Pale had so
shrunk that its southern boundary lay on the Dodder, and its
farthest limits were at Trim and Kells in Co. Meath.

Trim was maintained by virtue of the strength of its castle

and its importance as the head of a great honour; and also because it belonged to Richard Duke of York (father of Edward IV) who maintained independent state there between 1448 and 1460. Dublin and Trim were the headquarters from which he was able to launch his expeditions against the tottering England of Henry VI, whose effective rulers were Queen Margaret of Anjou, and Richard Neville the "King-maker" earl of Warwick. Trim, with its finely preserved castle, mediaeval church, abbey tower, walls, and other remains, and the nearby cathedral ruins at Newtown, is the most impressive relic of mediaeval Ireland; its walls enclose a distinctly larger area than those of Dublin itself, though Drogheda is a good deal larger still. The explanation probably lies in the fact that Dublin's walls were built so early that by the thirteenth century, when Drogheda (originally two separate towns) and Trim were walled, it had greatly outgrown its artificial limits. There is in fact documentary evidence that the area north of St. Audoen's and west of Parliament Street was enclosed with a wall for the first time about 1250.

I have already mentioned Dublin's water-supply, which was planned in 1244, and in operation within ten years. The mountain water, brought from the Dodder to the Poddle and thence by an artificial course to a basin by James's Street and so down to the New Gate, began to be piped to certain important users almost immediately. Before 1255 the Mayor and citizens granted to the Dominican friary liberty to lay a pipe through the city and across the river, providing they did no damage to the bridge, but the pipe's diameter was to be five inches, and the orifice for delivery of the water was to be so narrowed that "its opening may be stopped by the insertion of a man's little finger; and it shall at no time be larger". If the friars were to enlarge the pipe without the citizens' consent, their water would be cut off altogether. Sir Richard of Exeter, knight, was allowed to have a pipe the size of a goose-quill, taken to his house near the church of the Holy Trinity (Christ Church) for a rent of a chaplet of roses delivered each 24th of June. The city was paved between 1322 and 1329, a date which compares favourably with Southampton, 1384; Canterbury, 1474; and Bristol, the mother city, 1491.

The tale of Dublin's capture by Strongbow's knights can best be read in Gerald the Welshman's *History of the Conquest*.

The struggle was complicated by the many contending parties, for Hasculf, the Danish King, received assistance from the Irish of all parts of the country, as well as from Norwegians and Vikings from the Isles. The city was taken in 1170, but had to undergo three sieges in the following year, before the new owners were left in more or less quiet possession. Had the Danes and the several parties among the Irish had one concerted plan of action, and joined together in one siege, they could hardly have failed to uproot the invaders. On the day that Raymond le Gros and Milo de Cogan led their storming parties successfully into the city, a miracle occurred, for the Danish citizens found themselves unable to move a crucifix which they wished to take with them—their "luck" had departed.

Gerald, a great and lively writer, is full of picturesque touches: when Hasculf returned to besiege Dublin, his warriors were "armed in the Danish fashion, some having long breast-plates, and others shirts of mail; their shields were round, and coloured red, and were bound about with iron". He also relates a story of a band of Henry II's archers who in mid-winter went out to the village of Finglas foraging for fuel, and cut down a beautiful grove of ash and yew trees, which had been planted round the churchyard by the former abbot Kenach and other holy men. For this ecclesiastical and aesthetic sacrilege, the men were smitten with a pestilence. King Henry was holding his Christmas in a wickerwork (doubtless wattle-and-daub) palace, hurriedly built for him outside the eastern gate. "Very many of the princes of the land repaired to Dublin to visit the King's court, and were much astonished at the sumptuousness of his entertainments and the splendour of his household; and having places assigned them at the tables in the hall, by the King's command, they learnt to eat cranes which were served up, a food they before loathed."

Before the coming of the Anglo-Normans, Dublin was a city of the Danes, founded on the site of an earlier Irish centre soon after A.D. 845. It was a centre for raiding expeditions and a trading post, and its Kings were among the great heroes of the sagas; but their history of battles and explora-tion has not much to do with Dublin. Of all the battles the most epic was the victory of King Brian Boru over the Viking King Sigtryggr of the Silken Beard on Palm Sunday 1014,

154   Christ Church Cathedral, looking East

155   St. Patrick's Cathedral: south transept

157 St. Michan's Church: the mediaeval tower, with west doorway of 1686

156 St. Audoen's Church: the ruined chancel, c. 1455

on a spot somewhere near the present Mountjoy Square. The saga tells the immortal story of how, when the vikings were in flight, one of them named Thorstein stopped to tie his shoe-string, and his pursuer asked him why he did not fly as the rest did. "And he answered: 'Because I cannot get home to-night, for I am at home out in Iceland'; and his pursuer gave him peace." But in spite of this defeat, Sigtryggr still reigned in Dublin, and it was King Brian who was killed before the day was done.

Before the Vikings, Dublin lies under a cloud of myth and legend, with scraps of real history dimly showing through. We really know nothing except that a town and harbour worth fighting for were already well established by the second century A.D. Beyond this all is conjecture, apart from what the experts, Dr. George Little and others, can make of the names of the city. *Ath Clíath Duibhlinne*—the Ford of the Hurdles on Darkriverpool, we are told is the full and ancient name, with its alternative title *Druim Cuill Coille*—the Hazelwood Ridge. Not very enlightening, one might think; but at least it gives us one glimpse, clear and sharp in a diminishing crystal, of a little wood of nut-trees along a hill, the dark glowing water of the Annaliffey beneath, flowing down as it does still, and men coming and going at the ford, or struggling laden with burdens from the ships.

Bibliographical Note

This list includes only books of importance which have been largely consulted.

Chart, D. A.: *The Story of Dublin* ("Mediaeval Towns" series), rev. ed., 1932.

Cole, G. A. J. and Praeger, R. L.: *Handbook to the City of Dublin and Surrounding District* (British Association), 1908.

Cosgrave, D.: *North Dublin—City and Environs*, 2nd ed., n.d.

Georgian Society: *Records of Eighteenth-century Domestic Architecture and Decoration in Dublin*, 5 vols., 1909–13.

Gilbert, Sir J. T.: *A History of Dublin*, 3 vols., 1854–9.

Joyce, W. St. J.: *The Neighbourhood of Dublin*, 4th ed., 1939.

Malton, J.: *Picturesque and Descriptive View of the City of Dublin* . . . in 1791, 1792–99.

Maxwell, C.: *Dublin under the Georges*, 1714–1830, 3rd ed., 1946.

Saorstat Eireann Official Handbook, 1932.

Warburton, J., Whitelaw, J., and Walsh, R.: *A History of the City of Dublin*, 2 vols., 1818.

Though it appeared too late for consultation, the following important handbook must be added:

Wheeler, H. A. and Craig, M. J.: *The Dublin City Churches of the Church of Ireland*, 1948.

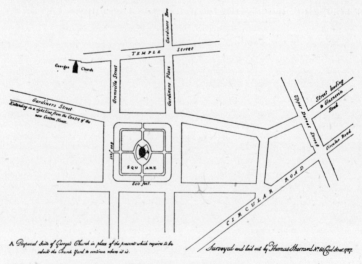

158 Original plan for Mountjoy Square, by Thomas Sherrard, 1787

159   St. Mary's Chapel of Ease, or the Black Church, 1829–30
John Semple, architect

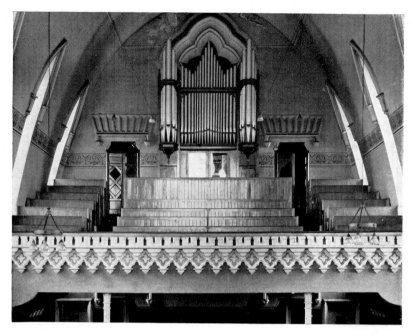

160   St. Mary's Chapel of Ease, or the Black Church, 1829–30
John Semple, architect

161   Catholic University Church, 1854–6
John Hungerford Pollen, architect

Notes to the Text

These notes are intended to give sources only for facts not easily accessible in books of general reference.

CHAPTER II

p. 27.　Irish railways—see Kevin Murray: "Dublin's First Railway", in *Dublin Historical Record*, I (1938–9), p. 19; "The Atmospheric Railway to Dalkey", *ibid.*, V (1942–3), p. 109; W. J. Gordon: *Our Home Railways*, I, pp. 55–60.

CHAPTER III

p. 43.　Plasterwork—see C. P. Curran: "Dublin Plaster Work", in *Journal of the Royal Society of Antiquaries of Ireland* LXX (7 S., X), 1940, p. 1 ff.

p. 48.　Edward Smyth—see H. G. Leask: "Dublin Custom House: The Riverine Sculptures", in *J.R.S.A.I.*, LXXV, 1945, p. 187 ff.

p. 49.　Trinity College front—see Constantia Maxwell in *Country Life*, 11 May 1945, p. 824–5.

p. 50.　Parliament House—see T. U. Sadleir: *Sir Edward Lovett Pearce*, 1927.

p. 53.　Portobello Harbour—see H. Phillips, "Early History of the Grand Canal", in *Dublin Hist. Rec.*, I (1938–9), p. 108 ff.; W. St. J. Joyce: *The Neighbourhood of Dublin*, 4th ed., 1939, p. 437 ff.; A. Peter: *Sketches of Old Dublin*, 1907, p. 237 ff.

p. 54.　Our Lady of Dublin—see Catriona MacLeod, "Some Late Mediaeval Wood Sculptures in Ireland", in *J.R.S.A.I.*, LXXVII, 1947, p. 53 ff.

p. 58.　St. Michan's—see W. F. Wakeman: *Old Dublin*, Second Series, 1887, p. 49.

p. 59.　Stoneybatter—see Dr. G. A. Little, "Pre-Norse Dublin", part II, in *Dublin Hist. Rec.*, VIII (1946), p. 92 ff.

CHAPTER IV

p. 63.　Irish land tenure—see Prof. James Hogan, "The Tricha Cét and related Land Measures", in *Proceedings of the Royal Irish Academy*, XXXVIII (1928–9), p. 148 ff. cf. Walter Map: *De Nugis Curialium*, Dist. II, xii.

p. 65.　Irish Open Fields—T. Kelly, "Some Rentals of the Earl of Shelburne's Estates, 1755–76", in *Dublin Hist. Rec.*, II (1939–40), p. 55 ff.; L. Ua Broin, "Rathcoole, Co. Dublin, and its Neighbourhood", in *J.R.S.A.I.*, LXXIII, 1943, p. 79 ff.; National Library of Ireland, Longfield Maps: Co. Dublin, vol. I, 75, 145; vol. II (Rathcoole); vol. III, 97. Compare Gudmund Hatt: "The Ownership of Cultivated Land" in *Det Kgl. Danske Videnskabernes Selskab*, Historisk-filologiske Meddelelser, XXVI, 6 (1939), esp. p. 6.

p. 72.　Railways—see note to p. 27.

CHAPTER V

p. 77.　Swift—see Denis Johnston, "The Mysterious Origin of Dean Swift", in *Dublin Hist. Rec.*, III (1940–1), p. 81 ff.

p. 83.　Woodward—C. P. Curran: "Benjamin Woodward, Ruskin and the O'Sheas", in *Studies*, XXIX (1940), p. 255 ff.

p. 86.　Statistics—mainly from *Reports and Printed Documents of the Corporation of Dublin*, vol. I, 1918, p. 81 ff. (Report No. 13 of the Housing Committee)—see also Civics Institute of Ireland: II, *The Dublin Civic Survey*, 1925; and Thom's *Directories* of Dublin (annual).

DUBLIN

p. 89.   Cassels—see C. P. Curran: *The Rotunda Hospital—its Architects and Craftsmen*, 1945.

p. 92.   Trinity College front—see note to p. 49.

Fitzwilliam estate—MS. plans in the possession of the Pembroke Estates Office, 1 Wilton Place, Dublin; and see E. Butler, "The Georgian Squares of Dublin", in *Country Life*, C, pp. 756, 810 ff., 25 Oct. and 1 Nov. 1946; F. A. Ashe, "Mountjoy Square", in *Dublin Hist. Rec.*, III (1940–1), p. 98 ff.

p. 93.   Francis Johnston—see John Betjeman's articles in *The Irish Builder*, LXXXIV, p. 121–2, 28 Mar. 1942; and in *The Pavilion*, ed. Myfanwy Piper, 1946; and *Irish Book-Lover*, XXVIII (1941–2), p. 115–16; Annals of Dublin by Owen Connellan, etc. (in *Directories*), s.a. 1836.

Street Lighting—see P. Meehan, "Early Dublin Public Lighting", in *Dublin Hist. Rec.*, V (1942–3), p. 130.

p. 95.   Plasterwork—see note to p. 43, and also C. P. Curran, "Cesare Ripa and the Dublin Stuccodores" in *Studies* XXVIII, 1939, p. 237 ff.; and "Michael Stapleton, Dublin Stuccodore", in *ibid.*, p. 439 ff.

p. 96.   Clanwilliam House—see C. P. Curran: *Nos. 85 & 86 St. Stephen's Green*, (1939).

p. 97.   Simpson's Hospital—R. Gahan, "Old Alms-Houses of Dublin", in *Dublin Hist. Rec.*, V (1942–3), p. 15 ff.; see also "Old Dublin Mansion-houses" in *The Irish Builder*, XXXV (1893), p. 69.

EPILOGUE

p. 100.   Jigginstown—see H. G. Leask: Irish Castles, 3rd ed.,1946, pp. 148–9.

Water-supply—see L. M. O'Brennan, "Little Rivers of Dublin", in *Dublin Hist. Rec.*, III (1940–1), p. 19 ff.

p. 101.   Potatoes—R. N. Salaman, "The Potato—Master or Servant?" in *New Biology*, ed. M. L. Johnson and M. Abercrombie, I, 1945, p. 9 ff.

p. 102.   Roll of Names, etc.—see J. T. Gilbert: *Historic and Municipal Documents of Ireland*, 1172–1320 (Rolls Series), 1870, p. 3 ff., 112 ff.

John of Corfe—*Rotulorum Patentium and Clausarum Cancellarii Hiberniae Calendarium*, ed. E. Tresham, I, part i, p. 38, 41. Adam Carleton—*Ibid.*, pp. 44–6, 61–2, 67, 69, 76, 79. John More—*Ibid.*, p. 82, 128.

p. 103.   Cistercian architecture—A. C. Champneys: *Irish Ecclesiastical Architecture*, 1910, esp. p. 232 ff.; H. G. Leask: *Jerpoint Abbey* (Official Guide); Conor O'Brien, "Jerpoint Abbey" in *The Architectural and Topographical Record*, I, 1908, p. 53 ff.

Christ Church, Dublin—E. H. Lewis-Crosby: *Christ Church Cathedral, Dublin—A Guide*; W. Butler: *The Cathedral Church of the Holy Trinity, Dublin*, 1901.

St. Patrick's—J. H. Bernard: *The Cathedral Church of St. Patrick*, rev. ed. 1940.

p. 104.   Dublin University—A. Gwynn, "The Mediaeval University of St. Patrick's, Dublin", in *Studies*, XXVII (1938), p. 199 ff.

p. 105.   Trim—see *Archaeological Journal*, LXXXVIII (1931), p. 364 ff.

Dublin—see J. L. J. Hughes, "Main Street, Dublin", in *Dublin Hist. Rec.*, III (1940–1), p. 67 ff.

Water supply—see note to p. 100; also J. T. Gilbert: *Calendar of Ancient Records of Dublin*, I, 1889, pp. 92, 101–2, 109.

p. 107.   The Names of Dublin—see G. A. Little, "Pre-Norse Dublin", in *Dublin Hist. Rec.*, VIII (1945–6), pp. 1, 92 ff.

Index

The captions of the plates are included; numerals in heavy type refer to the *figure numbers* of the illustrations.

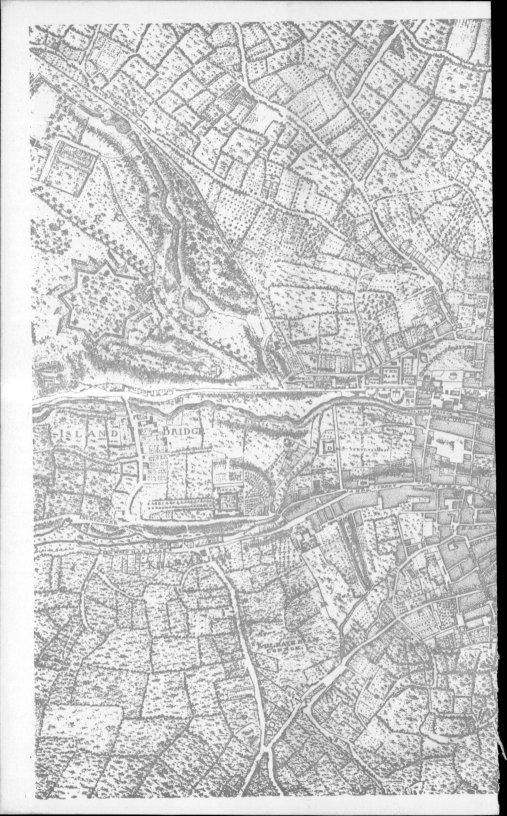